BACK TO THE HEART OF YOUTH WORK

Personal purity will always remain as a priority prerequisite to knowing God. Why? When we forfeit our godliness, we shatter our intimacy with Christ. The writer to the Hebrews clearly stated this principle: "Without holiness no one will see the Lord" (12:14, NIV). The psalmist lamented, "If I had cherished sin in my heart, the Lord would not have listened" (Psalm 66:18, NIV). We cannot afford to ignore the point of these verses—God does not walk with ungodly people.

The call of God resounds loud and clear:

> The eyes of the Lord move to and fro throughout the earth that He may strongly support those whose heart is completely His.
>
> 2 Chronicles 16:9

> Cease to do evil, learn to do good.
>
> Isaiah 1:16-17

> Let everyone who names the name of the Lord abstain from wickedness. . . . If a man cleanses himself from these things, he will be a vessel for honor, sanctified, useful to the Master, prepared for every good work.
>
> 2 Timothy 2:19, 21

We have been told that spiritual leadership depends upon communicative skill, vision, enthusiasm, organizational ability, personality, gifts, or raw guts. How often have we been reminded of the single most essential ingredient needed for being "useful to the Master"—personal purity?

You and I are called to exert a godly influence in a decadent society. We are called to set a godly standard in a very ungodly world. We are called to communicate a godly message to a sadly deceived people. Question: "How can we exert a godly influence if we ourselves are not godly?" Answer: "We can't." Question: "How [illegible] we set a godly standard if we ourselves are not godly?" An- [illegible] "We can't." Question: "How can we communicate a godly [illegible] if we ourselves are not godly?" Answer: "We can't."

[illegible]e forgotten what happened when Moses, in an act of high-ha[illegible]lful, defiant rebellion, struck a rock when he was told to speak to a rock and then took credit for the miraculous provision of water? "The Lord said to Moses and Aaron, 'Because you have not believed Me, to treat Me as holy in the sight of the sons of Israel, therefore you shall not bring this assembly into the land which I have given them" (Numbers 20:12).

Have we forgotten Uzzah, who, in direct disobedience to the command of God, reached out his hand to steady the ark as it bobbled on a wobbly cart? "And the anger of the Lord burned against Uzzah, and God struck him down there for his irreverence; and he died there by the ark of God" (2 Samuel 6:7).

Have we forgotten Saul, who acted in self-willed presumption, performing an act reserved only for the priest? "And Samuel said to Saul, 'You have acted foolishly; you have not kept the commandment of the Lord your God, which He commanded you, for now the Lord would have established your kingdom over Israel forever. But now your kingdom shall not endure. The Lord has sought out for Himself a man after His own heart, and the Lord has appointed him as ruler over His people, because you have not kept what the Lord commanded you' " (1 Samuel 13:13-14).

Have we forgotten our calling to be soldiers consumed with the task of pleasing the one who enlisted us? (2 Timothy 2:4) Have we forgotten that we must, as athletes, compete according to the rules? (2 Timothy 2:5) Have we forgotten that even the Apostle Paul exercised self-discipline lest, after having preached to others, he himself "should be disqualified"? (1 Corinthians 9:27)

Have we forgotten the truth of the words of Robert Murray M'Cheyne? "Do not forget the culture of the inner man—I mean of the heart. How diligently the cavalry officer keeps his sabre clean and sharp; every stain he rubs off with the greatest care. Remember, you are God's sword, His instrument—I trust, a chosen vessel unto Him to bear His name. In great measure, according to the purity and perfection of the instrument, will be the success. It is not great talents God blesses so much as likeness to Jesus. A holy minister is an awful weapon in the hand of God."*

Youth ministry involves far more than clever programming skills or charismatic personalities. Ministry begins with a heartfelt desire

---

*Quoted by Charles Haddon Spurgeon, *Lectures to My Students* (Grand Rapids, Michigan: Zondervan, 1954), p. 8.

to know God. The young people whom God has committed to our spiritual oversight will never develop such a heart if we do not possess one ourselves.

CHECKING YOUR HEART:
A Personal EKG

1. On paper honestly evaluate the quantity and quality of the time you currently spend in the Word of God each week. Is there any need for improvement? If so, what changes must be made?

2. Consider these suggestions that might make your time in the Word more productive and meaningful:

- **a.** Determine the time of day most conducive to an uninterrupted time in the Word.
- **b.** Build an altar. An altar is a place that is both private and free from distraction where you can meet with God one-on-one. Establish such a place and covenant with God that you will meet Him there.
- **c.** Select a book of the Bible that relates to a particular interest or need in your life.
- **d.** Set a realistic goal. One chapter per day might be appropriate. Far better to set a lesser goal and achieve it than strive for a greater goal and become frustrated over an inability to accomplish it!
- **e.** As you read, mark in the margin those verses which are especially meaningful to you.
- **f.** Keep a journal. A journal is a written response to the marked verses, usually worded as a prayer. It becomes a documentation of your spiritual journey. Such a record will prove to be a rich heritage to be passed on to others and will formulate the material from which your most meaningful messages will come.
- **g.** Walk with God. I mean this literally. Enoch walked with God and so do I. My richest times of prayer come as I take walks and visualize God walking right beside me. I am able to share with Him my deepest thoughts and emotions concerning every area of my life and the specific burdens He has laid on my

heart. By walking when I pray I find that my mind does not wander and I never fall asleep!

h. Don't allow your devotional time to become mechanical or routine. Relationships are dynamic, never static. Variety is the spice of life. Jesus Christ is a person to be known, not a mere concept to be understood. Enjoy Him. Allow yourself to experience the thrill of having a constant companion with whom you can share every moment of every day. He cares and understands. He has been there (Hebrews 4:15-16). He accepts you unconditionally. With Him you can be totally transparent all of the time. And as your walk develops, never allow yourself to lose the wonder of it all.

3. Evaluate the information that enters your eyes and ears. Consider the music to which you listen. Review the movies, videos, or television shows you watch. Do the magazines and books you read meet the standard of Philippians 4:8? If not, purpose in your heart that you will no longer defile yourself with mentally harmful material.

4. Get alone with the Lord right now and pray the words of Psalm 139:23-24: "Search me, O God, and know my heart; try me and know my anxious thoughts; and see if there be any hurtful way in me, and lead me in the everlasting way." Do any "little compromises" come to mind with which you must deal? If so, confess them as sin and experience His cleansing and deliverance.

5. As you contemplate your involvement in youth ministry, allow your own heart for knowing God to affect your goals for the young people whom you serve. Make it your greatest ambition to introduce young people to Jesus Christ and to enable them to get to know Him better. This desire should permeate every Bible study, social, camp, retreat, praise night, gathering—everything. The relationships you establish and the amount of energy you expend should now facilitate this all-consuming passion. Any lesser goal is unworthy of your time or effort.

2

"Pay Close Attention to Yourself" (Part 2)
Maintaining a Heart for Pleasing God

"Pay close attention to yourself" (1 Timothy 4:16).

"No soldier in active service entangles himself in the affairs of everyday life, so that he may please the one who enlisted him as a soldier" (2 Timothy 2:4).

"Well done, good and faithful slave" (Matthew 25:21).

Jesus' words in the twenty-fifth chapter of Matthew's Gospel summarize the greatest longing of my heart. My life can be reduced to one basic goal. I am a bondslave. Jesus Christ is my Master. The burning desire of my life is to "please the one who enlisted me." When I complete my life and God evaluates my ministry, I long to stand before my Lord and hear Him say to me, "Well done, good and faithful slave" (Matthew 25:21). Tragically, not everyone will hear those words. Not everyone will qualify as a "good and faithful slave." Will you? Will I?

We learn in athletics a principle that continually frightens me. "No one will ever remember how we begin; they will only remember how we end." Paul himself was tormented by that thought. In a most transparent moment, he bared his heart to the Corinthian church with the exhortation, "Do you not know that those who run in a race all run, but only one receives the prize? Run in such a way that you may win." He then confessed his greatest fear: "I buffet my body and make it my slave, lest possibly, after I have preached to others, I myself should be disqualified" (1 Corinthians 9:24, 27).

I want to end my life a winner. I am sure you do as well. The passion of my heart is to please Him in everything I do. Nothing else really matters.

We have been called by God to live a godly life and communicate a biblical message (1 Timothy 4:16). These two qualities provide the keys to effective youth ministry. A godly life is marked by a heart for knowing God. We shall now learn that a godly life is equally marked by a heart for pleasing God.

PLEASING GOD

What characterizes a person who pleases Jesus Christ? What does He look for? By what standard will He evaluate our lives? Once again, 1 Timothy 4 gives the answers.

1. Be committed to hard work (1 Timothy 4:10).

"For it is for this we labor" (1 Timothy 4:10). The word "labor" carries with it the idea of hard work. I know of no other way to achieve effective ministry. This same principle echoes from 2 Timothy 2:6: "The hard-working farmer ought to be the first to receive his share of the crops." You will find no room for laziness in the ministry. The work is at times relentless and overwhelming. If,

A BIBLICAL JOB DESCRIPTION

The responsibilities assigned to a youth pastor can seem overwhelming. Check this job description. He or she must:

- guard the flock (Acts 20:28);
- feed the flock (Acts 20:28);
- oversee the flock (Acts 20:28);
- agonize over the flock (Acts 20:31);
- know the flock (John 10:3);
- equip the flock (Colossians 1:28);
- reprove, rebuke, exhort the flock (2 Timothy 4:2);
- tenderly love the flock (1 Thessalonians 2:7);
- evangelize the world (2 Timothy 4:5);
- endure severe reactions (2 Timothy 4:3).

indeed, "the world is run by tired men," then those who serve in youth ministry lead the parade.

The freedom we enjoy as servants of Jesus Christ astounds me. As a rule, no one stands over our shoulders watching our every move. We do not punch in and punch out. We can basically come and go as we please. People mostly assume that if we are not around, we can be found attending an athletic event, doing some visitation, or hiding away for some uninterrupted study time.

Lazy people can get away with murder in the ministry. Many do just that—for a while. Sooner or later laziness will catch up with them. "Whatever your hand finds to do, verily, do it with all your might, for there is no activity or planning or wisdom in Sheol where you are going" (Ecclesiastes 9:10). Jesus said, "We must work the works of Him who sent Me, as long as it is day; night is coming, when no man can work" (John 9:4). Jesus committed Himself to hard work; so must we.

The volunteer staff doesn't have it any easier. These unsung heroes of the faith come alongside the youth pastor as they help to shoulder the work. For them too, youth ministry can be physically, mentally, emotionally, and spiritually draining and demanding. One who has a heart for pleasing Jesus Christ must be committed to hard work.

2. Dare to face opposition (1 Timothy 4:10).

The word *strive* in 1 Timothy 4:10 provides us with an exceedingly meaningful visual image. The Greek word refers to a hand-to-hand combat with no thought of retreat. Ours is an offensive campaign. God forbid that we should ever withdraw from the battle.

Youth ministry, by its very nature, must involve itself with issues colored with extreme controversy. Touching the lives of the young people in our society causes us to encounter such realities as divorce, child abuse, immorality, homosexuality, drug abuse, abortion, suicide, and so on. As youth workers, we are called to lead young people out of the caverns of their own confusion concerning these subjects. No one said it would be easy.

God speaks to an overwhelmingly confused generation of young people. His voice sounds clear and absolute. It also offends. Paul referred to "the offense of the cross" (Galatians 5:11, NIV). The raw reality of the situation can be simply stated: God's truth, when declared without compromise, will generate waves of reaction.

- "And about that time there arose no small disturbance concerning the Way" (Acts 19:23).
- "And all the city was aroused" (Acts 21:30).
- "And as he said this, there arose a dissension" (Acts 23:7).
- "And there arose a great uproar" (Acts 23:9).

Proclaiming truth has always had the same result. It always will. The individual who desires to please Jesus Christ must be resolute in his heart that he will never back down nor shrink from the conflict.

Boldness in the face of opposition must characterize our teaching and our lifestyles. We must share the commitment of Daniel, who "made up his mind that he would not defile himself" (Daniel 1:8). We can do no less than Shadrach, Meshach, and Abednego, who boldly declared, "God . . . is able to deliver us from the furnace of blazing fire. . . . But even if He does not, let it be known to you, O king, that we are not going to serve your gods or worship the golden image that you have set up" (Daniel 3:17-18).

Are there any modern-day Daniels who would dare defy a decree outlawing prayer to the one true God? "Now when Daniel knew that the document was signed, he entered his house (now in his roof chamber he had windows open toward Jerusalem); and he continued kneeling on his knees three times a day, praying and giving thanks

LIVING OBJECT LESSONS

First Timothy 4:12 lists five specific areas in which we are to be examples:

- the way we talk ("speech");
- the way we live ("conduct");
- the way we relate to others ("love");
- the way we relate to God ("faith");
- the way we relate to members of the opposite sex ("purity").

before his God, as he had been doing previously" (Daniel 6:10).

We face a leadership crisis because of compromise, both within and without the Church. But the servant who pleases Jesus Christ is not afraid to stand for the truth. "For God has not given us a spirit of timidity, but of power and love and discipline" (2 Timothy 1:7).

3. Show yourself an example (1 Timothy 4:12). Ministry is, first and foremost, modeling. "Like people, like priest," Hosea declared (Hosea 4:9). The people reflected their leaders. The same is true today. How sobering to realize that the young people we seek to influence will likely never achieve a higher level of spiritual commitment than that reflected in our lives. With this thought in mind Jeremiah warned, "Cursed be the one who does the Lord's work negligently" (Jeremiah 48:10). A leader cannot possibly be effective unless he can say to his people, "Be imitators of me, just as I also am of Christ" (1 Corinthians 11:1). How imperative that we be able to exhort the young people committed to our care, "Join in following my example, and observe those who walk according to the pattern you have in us" (Philippians 3:17). Timothy was commanded to show himself "an example of those who believe" (1 Timothy 4:12). This command applies to us as well.

If the message we communicate to our young people becomes the old standard, "Do as I say, not as I do," we should do our students a favor and get out of youth ministry. A life of such hypocrisy will never be pleasing to the Christ who calls upon us to be examples. Remember four profound words that should concern every one of us who serve in a place of spiritual influence: "Like people, like priest."

4. Live for the purpose of communicating truth (1 Timothy 4:13).

We have on our hands a totally secularized generation. God no longer has a place within the thinking of the majority of today's teenagers. They have become practical atheists, living their lives as if God didn't exist. Paul's indictment of his society applies equally to ours: "There is no fear of God before their eyes" (Romans 2:24).

These words are no hyperbole. I asked a class of graduating seniors this question: "In your opinion, who is Jesus Christ?" The class concluded: "Jesus Christ was some religious guy who lived 200 years ago." They thought of Him as a contemporary of George Washington. I know of a young man who, until I met him, had heard of Jesus Christ only in the context of a swearword, with absolutely no comprehension of Him as a person. I am not describing life in an isolated jungle or an uncharted wilderness. These young people live within ten minutes of my house.

You and I are nothing less than cross-cultural missionaries, naming the name of Christ where He has never been named before. A heart that seeks to please Christ burns with a desire to read the Word ("give attention to the public reading of Scripture"), apply the Word ("to exhortation"), and explain the Word ("and teaching").

Consider your role within youth ministry. Some are called and gifted to teach. Most are not. Yours may be a behind-the-scenes, support ministry. If so, I thank God for you. These who are called upon to carry the teaching responsibilities could not possibly do what they do without a loyal and faithful support team behind them. Never view your involvement as unimportant, insignificant, or second-class. Your work, no matter how miniscule it may seem in terms of its importance, facilitates the teaching. In your own way you contribute to the overall goal of allowing God to have a voice. View it that way. See the big picture. The servant who pleases Jesus Christ understands that he is not just blowing up rafts for the upcoming river-rafting trip or buying Cokes for the beach barbeque. Not by a long shot. The servant of Jesus Christ understands that she is helping to change the destiny of the world. Her tasks are contributing to the overall goal of allowing God to have a voice to a generation that has never heard Him speak before.

5. View the ministry for what it is, a gift (1 Timothy 4:14).

I would die if I could no longer do what I do. Youth ministry has become the burning passion of my heart, my all-consuming desire. I view this responsibility as of gargantuan proportion; for this reason I shake. I consider ministry a priceless privilege; for this reason I rejoice. Youth ministry is indeed God-given, a "spiritual gift."

Those two words, "spiritual gift," have confused many people. They do not specifically refer to a spiritual gift proper, such as those listed in Romans 12. Rather, they generally refer to anything given to us by God. Paul uses the same words in Romans 1:11: "For I long to see you in order that I may impart some spiritual gift to you." God bestowed the gift upon Timothy "with the laying on of hands by the presbytery" (1 Timothy 4:14), a reference to his ordination to the Gospel ministry. The point should be obvious. The privilege of ministry is a gift given to us by God, a gift which must be respected and guarded.

Disqualification can come too quickly to one who would squander this privilege through personal compromise. The servant who pleases Jesus Christ, recognizing how easy it is to forfeit the gift of ministry, takes every precaution to guard what has been entrusted. Would you be a pleasing servant? "Run in a such a way that you may win" (1 Corinthians 9:24).

6. Be constantly maturing (1 Timothy 4:15).

"Take pains with these things [the principles listed in 1 Timothy 4]; be absorbed in them, so that your progress may be evident to all." I find this instruction incredibly comforting. If it were not recorded within the pages of Scripture, I would not be in youth ministry today.

The standard has been defined. It is sky-high, and rightly so. The lines must be drawn at the level of the leader. Ours is certainly the "stricter judgment" (James 3:1). Ours are the lives by which those who follow measure their own. Yet none of us consistently lives up to this standard all of the time. None of us. Having set the standard by which we evaluate our lives, Paul clearly explains exactly what

God expects—not the *perfection* of our lives but the *direction* of our lives. Are we progressing toward the attainment of this standard? If so, then from God's perspective we are right on target. If not, some radical changes must be made.

I want to be a man whose heart yearns to know God. I long to be a man whose heart aches with a desire to please God. Such a person continually heeds the command, "Pay close attention to yourself." Having gained an understanding of all that this exhortation entails, we shall, in the next chapter, turn our attention to a biblical message by learning how to "pay close attention to (our) teaching."

CHECKING YOUR HEART:
A Personal EKG

1. The demands of youth ministry do not allow us the luxury of wasted time. Youth ministry is hard work, plain and simple. Time management, therefore, becomes of monumental importance for the youth worker, whether full- or part-time, professional or volunteer. Taking this premise into consideration, honestly consider these questions:

- **a.** What are your personal priorities? Give this question some serious thought. Time management hinges on its answer.
- **b.** In terms of the allotment of your time, are these priorities receiving an ample amount of quality time, or are they being neglected for lesser pursuits?
- **c.** Are there any regular activities in your life that could be considered as wasted time?
- **d.** Keep an hourly account of your time expenditures this week. You may be very surprised as you learn where the bulk of your time goes. At the end of the week, evaluate your findings in order to determine if a reordering of your life is necessary.
- **e.** If you routinely find yourself too busy to accomplish any task with excellence, determine that you will begin to do a few things with excellence rather than many things with mediocrity. What activities or pursuits will you need to give up in order to do a few things with excellence?

f. Get yourself a month-at-a-glance calendar and begin to visualize every commitment in the context of the two weeks immediately preceding and following each event. Before you agree to any new tasks, ask yourself and your family if you can handle another duty. If not, without feeling guilty, say no.

2. Willingness to stand alone characterizes anyone who would please Jesus Christ. In what areas are you taking some heat? How are you handling these situations? Have you faithfully and tactfully held your ground, or have you buckled under the pressure and compromised?

When you do stand alone, record the incident in a journal. You will thereby develop a rich spiritual heritage that can be passed on to your children or the young people to whom you minister. If you routinely fall in the face of flak, find someone you respect, explain the situation, ask for prayer support, and allow him or her to hold you accountable. The fact that you will have to report every time you back down will itself become a motivation for you to stand.

3. An exemplary life is a powerful life. An exemplary life reveals an inward quality that I like to call "integrity." What is integrity? I picture integrity as someone standing in front of any group of people anywhere, anytime, and allowing them to ask anything they want about his or her personal, private life. Integrity is the ability to answer every question honestly, without being ashamed. Can you do that? Could someone ask something about your speech, conduct, love, faith, or purity that might cause you embarrassment? If so, pinpoint the area and do a personal Bible study regarding the subject. Commit the key verses to memory and ask a close friend to periodically ask you pointed, probing questions concerning your areas of weakness.

4. As you fulfill your job description, what are you accomplishing? I hope you immediately thought of this answer: "I am changing the destiny of the world." If you didn't, think through how your task contributes to the overall priority of facilitating the teaching.

Do you feel frustrated, thinking that you are merely spinning your wheels, accomplishing nothing of lasting value? If so, set up an appointment with the one under whose leadership you are serving and express your concerns. Perhaps that person can help you to better visualize the whole picture. Perhaps a redefining of duties will allow you to more directly contribute to the priority of giving God a voice.

5. Is your ministry a privilege or a pain, a delight or a drudgery? Reread 1 Timothy 4:14 and begin to visualize youth ministry for what it is: a God-given gift, granted to but a select few. Take out a sheet of paper and write down all of the positive benefits that have come to your life because of your unspeakable privilege of influencing a desperately needy generation.

6. Do you ever feel inadequate to the task because of personal inconsistencies? Join the club; none of us walks on water. First Timothy 4 sets the standard. Don't expect perfection, but see to it that the direction of your life moves toward the standard.

How are you doing? Think back to where you were one year ago. Can you see any changes? Ask some of those closest to you if they have seen any evidence of maturity in your life. Now that the standard is firmly fixed in your mind, set some personal goals in relation to the areas requiring improvement. What steps can you take to begin to achieve those goals? A journal is invaluable at this point.

Write down on paper exactly what you want to change. Evaluate your life in one month and note any progress that has been made. Do not allow temporary failure to discourage or defeat you. The Christian life is always two steps forward and one step back. Failure is not falling down. Failure comes from staying down once you have fallen. When you blow it, pick yourself back up, confess your sin, and keep on moving. "Take pains with these things; be absorbed in them, so that your progress may be evident to all" (1 Timothy 4:15).

3

"Pay Close Attention to Your Teaching" (Part 1)

Maintaining a Heart for Communicating Truth

"Pay close attention to . . . your teaching" (1 Timothy 4:16).

Preach the Word; be ready in season and out of season; reprove, rebuke, exhort, with great patience and instruction" (2 Timothy 4:2).

Preaching has become the lost art of our day. I have received too many letters from too many young people bemoaning the fact that their pastor bores them or that their youth pastor teaches only the basics. What an inexpressible tragedy! It's the old story: no one has ever come close to reasoning me out of my faith, but I have nearly been bored out of my faith many times. If the Word of the living God is itself "living and active and sharper than any two-edged sword" (Hebrews 4:12), then it should be proclaimed that way. Too often, it is not. Preaching has indeed become the lost art of our day.

We can identify several reasons for this. First, many speakers have been deluded into thinking that young people cannot handle, or are not interested in, hearing truth. Yet, virtually every young person I meet is crying out for answers. A second reason is that many in the ministry simply do not want to pay the price required to deliver solid, relevant, gripping messages. How much easier to plan a party than prepare a sermon! A third reason is that skillful communicative technique takes time and effort to develop. It comes from a concerted effort to scrutinize and evaluate skilled communicators. Personal practice and honest self-evaluation are indispensable when it comes to developing one's own unique communicative style. Very few pursue the ability to communicate or see it as a goal worthy of their time or attention.

A skilled communicator seeks to persuade—never to manipulate. The difference between manipulation and persuasion arises out of the purity of one's motive. If a speaker desires to move a crowd in order to achieve his own ends, he manipulates. If he seeks to motivate people in order to glorify God and improve the lives of those to whom he speaks, he persuades. Paul wrote, "Knowing the fear of the Lord, we persuade men" (2 Corinthians 5:11). Agrippa said to Paul, "In a short time you will persuade me to become a Christian" (Acts 26:28). Always see the goal of effective communication as persuasion.

If you desire to improve this facet of your life and ministry, this chapter will prove helpful. Two aspects will be discussed: the right method and the right mechanics.

THE RIGHT METHOD

Consider two types of messages customarily used in youth ministry, both equally important. We commonly refer to them as the topical message and the expository message.

The topical message deals with a specific subject, utilizing information from the Bible as a whole. This method allows for as comprehensive a study of a given topic as possible. Any typical teenage trauma can be turned into a timely topical treatment. Such subjects might include dating, spiritual warfare, family life, friendships, apologetics, Satan, end times, prayer, or witnessing. When I served as a youth pastor, I generally used topical messages during our midweek Bible study, characteristically the time most first-time visitors came. Publicizing the topics in advance was easy, generating great excitement. Teaching in a three- to six-week series format allowed for an even fuller discussion of every aspect of the topic at hand.

An expository message deals with a specific text of Scripture. The theme and outline must come from the text itself. Scriptural material from outside the text can be used, but only for illustrative or explanatory purposes. From expository messages our young people perceive the Bible as more than a collection of verses or one-liners. The books of the Bible have a flow, a continuity to them. Expository preaching accurately and effectively communicates this reality.

How does the preparation of these two types of messages differ? Since the topical message tends to be the easier of the two, we shall begin our discussion here.

PREPARING A TOPICAL MESSAGE

Begin by selecting a topic. A group-wide survey assessing the needs of the group as a whole is invaluable at this point. Once you have chosen the topic, ask these questions: who, what, where, when, why, and how? These questions will determine the outline of the series as well as the outline of each individual message within the series.

This who-what-where-when-why-and-how method also works for each individual message. The outline of the message on the physical aspects of dating might flow something like this: I. Why is sex such an explosive subject among young people today? II. What is God's standard regarding the physical aspect of dating? III. What are the consequences of violating that standard? IV. What should you do if you have already blown it? (Appendices A and B contain a more fully developed outline for a topical message and a sample topical

OUTLINING A SERIES

If you are developing a series on the subject of dating, you could use the who-what-where-when-why-and-how method to break the series down in this way:

- Week 1: "Why Date?" Consider five purposes God wants to accomplish in dating.
- Week 2: "Whom Should I Date?" Build a case for only dating a growing believer, and consider the pros and cons of going steady.
- Week 3: "How Should I Date?" Discuss the proper manners to be used on a date, the correct way to ask a date out, responsibilities to the parents of the date, etc.
- Week 4: "How Should I Date? part 2" The physical aspect of dating would be the topic of discussion, including the age-old question, "How far can I go?"
- Week 5: "What Is Genuine Love?" The Bible clearly defines the characteristics of genuine love. A study of 1 Corinthians 13 would make up the bulk of this message.
- Week 6: "What Is God's Timing for Engagement?" The series would conclude with eight prerequisites that should be realized before a person becomes engaged.

teaching schedule.)

The strength of the topical message stems from the ease with which we can cover a subject comprehensively in a relatively small amount of time. But avoid one weakness—the tendency to fabricate the outline first and then find Scripture verses to fit it. The topical message, if done correctly, will require a great deal of discipline in study and a passion for communicating the Word with accuracy. As an absolute essential, make every point within the outline strictly biblical.

PREPARING AN EXPOSITORY MESSAGE

The expository message can be a little more tricky. While the entire Bible can be used for the purposes of illustration and explanation, the theme and every major point in the outline must come from one text. Several principles must be strictly adhered to for one to be considered an accurate expositor.

1. Brush up on the background.

Every book in the Bible was written for a specific purpose (often called the "occasion" of the book) during a specific time period. The cultural setting and occasion must be known if the book is to be interpreted properly. A good Old and New Testament introduction or critical commentary should provide all the background material needed.

2. Consider the context.

Look for a definite flow to each book. Every paragraph must be seen in its relationship to the material immediately preceding and following it. To isolate a passage from its context is a grievous crime. Such "proof-texting" can result in our making the Bible say anything we want it to say. "(Judas) went away and hanged himself " (Matthew 27:5), "Go and do the same" (Luke 10:37), and "What you do, do quickly" (John 13:27) were never meant to flow together!

3. Test out the theme.

Express the theme in a one-sentence summary of the passage being studied. Note, please, that every verse within the passage must be directly or indirectly related to the theme. The violation of this principle will result in an invalid theme.

No doubt you will wonder, "How many verses should I deal with each week?" I can offer no hard and fast rule. Two factors will come into play. How many weeks do you want to spend in a given book? How many verses do you need to consider before you can come up with a valid, relevant theme? Please be certain, however, that you guard against an arbitrary division of the book. Your passage divisions must reflect the natural outline of the book itself. (Appendix D contains a sample expository teaching schedule.) The hot tip at this point: invest in a good study Bible.

4. Prioritize the principles.

Study each verse within the passage. Arrive at an accurate understanding of the author's message. Each verse or section of verses should be rewritten as a principle: a statement of truth that is always true, no matter when stated. Principles are absolute, timeless, and relevant to today. "Noah took two of every kind of animal into the ark" is a statement of fact but not a principle, since Noah is no longer taking two of every kind of animal into an ark. That fact has no bearing on life today in terms of what we believe (convictions) or how we live (character). But consider this: "God has an intolerance of sin and will severely judge it." That enunciates a principle. "God's patience toward a sinner may at some point run out." Another statement cast as a principle. Both were true in Noah's day and both are equally true and applicable to our lives today.

Since we have only a finite amount of time in which to communicate our message, the principles within a given passage must be prioritized. We cannot possibly give out everything our study has uncovered. Only the most important will be developed. The priority principles will be determined by the thrust and direction of the passage coupled with the needs of the young people to whom we are speaking.

5. Agonize over the application.

The entire message builds to this pinnacle. At this point the expositor tells the listener what to do in response to the truth just learned. Practical in its orientation, the application summarizes the verdict toward which the speaker builds throughout the message.

AN EXPOSITORY OUTLINE

The outline holds a place of prominence as one of the most essential dimensions of sermon preparation. The outline is to the sermon what a road map is to a vacation. The outline gives a sense of organization and progression to a message. Of paramount importance, the outline must be clear and concise. (See Appendix C for a sample expository outline.) The outline consists of three distinct parts: the introduction, body, and conclusion.

1. The introduction

Effective communicators accomplish several goals within the first few minutes of the message. As a speaker, you must:

- Establish credibility. You must answer the question, "Why

should we listen to you?" Statistics, stories, or personal experiences should convey your qualification to address the issues at hand.

- Build rapport with the audience. A statement communicating some kind of identification with the group being addressed is very helpful if not essential.
- Capture the attention of your audience. As people arrive, their minds for the most part are not focused on the lesson about to be given. They are thinking about school, problems at home, pressures, the football game Friday night, a boyfriend or girlfriend, etc. To be an effective communicator, you must gather up all of those disjointed thoughts and zero them in on your message. The very first sentence out of your mouth becomes by far the most important.
- State your theme. If after the introduction has been completed the young people still have no clue as to the subject at hand, you will have failed most miserably. The impact of the remainder of the message depends on your ability to clearly define your subject and direction.
- Build anticipation for what follows next. A good communicator will begin by carefully creating a sense of conflict, tension, or identification in the minds of the young people regarding the subject at hand. You must clearly indicate that the conflict will be resolved within the body of the message. To the degree that you are successful in "setting up" a message, to that degree the young people will be locked in, anxiously awaiting what comes next.

2. The body

The body contains the bulk of the message. Here the speaker takes on the character of a prosecuting attorney in front of a jury, driving for a verdict, "Guilty as charged." In the body, you will accomplish the following:

- Support the theme. Having established your theme in the introduction, you will now give all of your lines of reasoning and evidence as discovered in your study. The evidence will consist of clearly defined points of truth (principles). Each point must balance the others while building to a crescendo or climax. Every message must present a sense of logical progression. You wish to present an ironclad case. Your study of a passage or topic should be so thorough that, while not everyone may agree with you, no one will be able to prove you wrong.

● Develop the principles. Every point in the outline must be hard-hitting. This comes about by virtue of the fact that you will have prioritized the principles and will present only the most important. You will explain, amplify, and illustrate each point. When the body of the message concludes, the theme of the message will have been clearly understood and properly defended. All who have heard the message will now know exactly what they should believe and why they should believe it.

3. The conclusion

In the introduction, the speaker tells his audience what he is going to say. In the body, he says it. In the conclusion, he tells them what he has just said. If done correctly, no one can possibly miss the point. In the conclusion:

● Review the theme. Stated in the introduction and supported in the body, the theme will now be reviewed in the conclusion. The attorney will address the jury with this impassioned plea: "Based upon what you have just heard, I submit to you, men and women of this jury, that the defendant is guilty as charged."

● Drive the theme home. At this juncture you will give a final sense of urgency to the whole message. If you haven't convinced your audience by now, you will either sell it here or forget it.

● Stir your listeners to action. Some would call this the application: a specific discussion concerning the listeners' proper response to what they have just heard. Consisting of very practical steps of action, a good conclusion will allow the listeners to know exactly what they must do when they get home.

We have considered only one half of the communicative process. We can have the best content in the world and organize it perfectly. If we fail to express the message effectively, our goal of persuasion will not be achieved. We must now turn our attention to the mechanics of effective communication.

THE RIGHT MECHANICS

We are dealing with this problem: the average attention span of a young person is somewhere between five to seven seconds. Generally, in only five to seven seconds, his mind begins to wander. Any distraction, such as a passing car, a sneeze, the buzz of a fly, will shift his attention.

To complicate the problem, the better you communicate, the more difficulty you may have in holding your audience. Why? As you communicate a thought, you may trigger a tangential thought, causing the young person to dwell on or comment about the ideas that just popped into his head. Adults, unfortunately, seem no better. We have all experienced the reality of the wandering mind. This happens no matter how disciplined a listener we may consider ourselves.

Is there any hope of holding an audience? Certainly. At our fingertips we can find five techniques to capture and maintain the attention of an audience.

1. Vocabulary

A communicator uses words as an artist uses paint. The words we use should paint mental images, enabling our listeners to accurately visualize everything we are trying to communicate. With a variety of colors on her palette, a skilled painter has no limit to the beauty she can create on her canvas. And so with the verbal communicator.

The best way to build a vocabulary is to read. Such a discipline will result in a plethora of words at our disposal. We will also be exposed to a wealth of material from which we can illustrate a variety of principles.

Off-color words should never be used. These will only build a wall

POWER WORDS

Certain words have what I like to call "potency." These words immediately arrest the attention of an audience the moment the speaker utters them. Such words as *violently, devastating, incredible, tremendous, paralyzing, enormous, crushing, insipid, invariably,* and *sensational* I consider as potent words. Use them like salt: just enough to season the message, but not so much that they destroy its flavor.

between a speaker and the audience. The principle to follow: when in doubt, don't.

We should be alert to similes, metaphors, and hyperbole. A simile compares two things using the words *like* or *as*. A metaphor is a comparison that does not use the words *like* or *as*. An hyperbole is a purposeful exaggeration used to make a point.

Jesus was the master communicator. He painted vivid mental images. "The kingdom of heaven is like a mustard seed" (Matthew 13:31) illustrates the use of the simile. Read Matthew 13:3-8 as an incredible usage of metaphor. Our Lord used a brilliant metaphor in Luke 12:1: "Beware of the leaven of the Pharisees, which is hypocrisy." Paul used three metaphors in describing a Christian. Can you pick them out in 2 Timothy 2:4-7? An example of hyperbole can be seen in Matthew 18:22: "Jesus said to him, 'I do not say to you, up to seven times, but up to seventy times seven." A Pauline example can be seen in 1 Corinthians 13:1-3.

2. Voice

Every time you vary your voice when speaking, you succeed in grabbing your listeners and focusing their attention on what you are saying. The proper use of the voice can itself assist in helping a listener to visualize what is being described.

Three qualities can be varied endlessly: volume, rate of speech, and pitch. The key ingredient—consistency. Your voice must be consistent with the message you are communicating. As a rule, in describing an exciting scene, your voice should get faster, louder, and higher. To describe a serious scene, drop the volume, become hushed or muted in tone, and slow the pace. For emphasis, you might become very staccato, or you may decide to put it in high gear and then, suddenly, drop your rate of speech and tone. Try it sometime. You will notice that at the precise moment of change every head in the place will turn your way to see what has happened.

3. Gestures

The use of hand gestures enables you to paint visual images to accompany the mental images your words convey. You can beat out a sentence for emphasis. You can picture a burst of light by extending your fingers and moving your hands in an outward motion.

Images of peaceful tranquility can be communicated by describing a placid lake while illustrating the smoothness of the water with the palms down, hands together at the belt buckle, and then moving them outward from the body. Once again, consistency becomes the key ingredient.

Gestures must be appropriate to the crowd and room size. The smaller the crowd, the more the gestures will stay within the width of the body. The larger the crowd, the more they will extend away from the body. But above all, they must be as natural as possible so as to not become distracting through overuse.

4. Facial expressions

Our faces can express every possible human emotion, from terror to sheer exhilaration. Your face should generally reflect an open and

SALTING THE LISTENER'S OATS

"You can lead a horse to water but you can't make him drink." I would add, "Unless you put salt in his oats." Salting a listener's oats refers to a speaker's ability to create a thirst for what is unfolding. Used correctly, this technique will cause an audience to sit on the edge of their seats, anxiously awaiting the very next words to be uttered. It is skillful communication at its best.

"Let me share with you the most important single principle I have ever learned relative to effective communication. This one principle brought about the most dramatic change to ever take place in my life. If I had not learned this principle, I would not be in youth ministry today. Would you like me to tell you?" If the word *yes* just popped into your mind, I just now succeeded in salting the oats.

Avoid one danger in using this technique. Make certain that you deliver what you have promised. If you have guaranteed a life-changing principle, you had better come up with one. To build up your listeners only to let them down produces enormous frustration and a credibility gap that may never be bridged.

pleasant countenance while expressing the emotion or intensity of the message.

Eyes afford the most communicative part of the face. They are, after all, the windows of the soul. Eye contact will reduce a mass of people to individuals. Through the use of your eyes you can communicate interest in the individual and create the perception that you are talking directly to each one present.

5. The dramatic pause

Can you imagine the impact of a speaker moving along at high speed and then suddenly, without warning—stopping, just for a moment, before making a very important statement? The sudden silence would arrest the attention of everyone in the house. The effectiveness of the dramatic pause depends upon timing. To produce the desired effect, the pause must be placed immediately in front of or after an incredibly important thought.

SOME FINAL TIPS

We have just taken a glimpse at both the method and mechanics of effective communication. Let me suggest a couple of additional thoughts.

Skillful communication will, with sufficient practice, become a way of life. Though the implementation of these techniques may seem cumbersome at first, given enough time their use will become as natural to you as breathing.

Communication style can be developed. As with any art, practice makes perfect. Sure, gifts and temperament have a part to play. But any of us, regardless of gifts or personality, can improve. I would suggest studying people you consider to be exceptional communicators. Dissect them, pick them apart, evaluate everything they do. You don't wish to become a carbon copy, but to emulate those qualities that will make you as effective as you can be.

Use a cassette recorder. Tape every message you give and critique yourself in terms of the mechanics discussed here. Did you use the dramatic pause effectively? How about your words: can you improve in your selection? Did you vary your voice effectively and at points salt the listener's oats? You might send the tapes to someone you respect for constructive criticism.

Nothing good ever comes cheap. But after fifteen years of youth ministry experience, I can assure you that any time and effort invested in the process will pay incredible dividends for literally decades to come. The world belongs to communicators.

CHECKING YOUR HEART:
A Personal EKG

1. Becoming a good communicator begins by being a good listener. Begin this Sunday by outlining every message you hear. See if you can determine when the introduction ends and the body begins. When does the speaker move into the conclusion? What was the first sentence? Did the speaker succeed in capturing your attention? Make a list of the characteristics of the introduction, body, and conclusion and check them off as they appear in the message.

2. Select a short epistle and mark off the major outline divisions. Read and reread one section at a time as you discover the theme. Go back over every verse and ask yourself how each one relates directly or indirectly to your one-sentence summary of the passage. Rephrase each verse as a principle. You won't find this easy. Having taught a college-level course for years on the subject of sermon preparation, I can testify that outlining stands as the single most difficult task for my students. Practice makes perfect, so hang in there and don't give up.

3. Make a list of the five topics that you might use as a short series. Using the who-what-where-when-why-and-how approach, write down three to five individual messages you could develop for each topic.

4. Get alone with a tape recorder and practice telling a story. You might feel more comfortable reading one. Begin with a child's storybook. Practice voice inflections as you dramatize the story. Play the tape back and, with your eyes closed, see if you can picture the action.

5. Critique someone whom you consider to be a good communicator. Use the techniques listed under "The Right Mechanics" as your guide. Benefit from good examples while learning to avoid the mistakes of bad examples.

6. Spend two or three hours in the magazine section of your library. Read in a variety of areas. What quotes, one-liners, or stories can you use in the coming week as illustrations of something you are trying to communicate? Can you make two or three hours a weekly goal?

7. Set a realistic reading goal of perhaps one book per month. Make a commitment that you will look up every unfamiliar word. In this way, over a period of time, you will build a very workable vocabulary. (For good measure, you will probably start tearing up the league when it comes to a good game of Scrabble!) Have fun. Reading should never be a drudgery, but one of life's greatest pleasures.

8. Developing the art of effective communication constitutes one of the greatest adventures possible. Enjoy every second of this lifelong pursuit!

4

"Pay Close Attention to Your Teaching" (Part 2)

Maintaining a Heart for Creative Communication

"And according to Paul's custom, he went to them, and for three Sabbaths reasoned with them from the Scriptures" (Acts 17:2).

"And we proclaim Him, admonishing every man and teaching every man with all wisdom, that we may present every man complete in Christ. And for this purpose also I labor" (Colossians 1:28-29).

"Dewey, listen: whatever you do in choosing a career, do *not* go into public speaking." With those words, my tenth-grade drama teacher permanently etched herself into my past. Oh, her comments got better than that. "In the fifteen years I have taught drama," she proclaimed, "you are the single most boring student I have ever had!" How's that for a rather ominous, inauspicious introduction to the realm of public speaking? The giving of a speech may not be for everyone.

Do you want to have some fun? Compile a list of six or eight common fears that people have. Ask your friends to list them in their order of priority. An acquaintance of mine did just that, and I could not believe his results. The fear of heights ranked as the number-three fear of most of the people asked. Death ranked number two. Do you have any idea what ranked number one? Giving a speech. That's right. While I would not call his findings conclusive, they certainly do underscore one startling fact: among his friends anyway, people would rather die than give a speech!

In the last chapter, I outlined in detail the principles resulting in effective speech delivery. As you read them, how did you feel? Inspired? Challenged? Ready to have at 'em? Or were you terrified at the thought of standing up in front of a group of people (teenagers, no less!) and opening your mouth? Public speaking is certainly not everyone's cup of tea.

Our objective in teaching will always remain the same: "And we proclaim Him, admonishing every man and teaching every man with all wisdom, that we may present every man complete in Christ" (Colossians 1:28). The means to achieving this end will always be varied. Ah, yes, variety is indeed the spice of life.

The lecture certainly has its place in youth ministry. Goals can be accomplished through persuasive preaching that can never be realized through any other means. The creative teacher, however, will package his message in a variety of ways.

CREATIVE TEACHING TECHNIQUES

Let's consider a few approaches in order to stimulate your own thinking. But please remember, no matter what means you may choose, there will never be any substitute for proper preparation and accurate biblical exposition. The principles of lesson preparation and interpretation that you have learned in the preceding chapter

A CASE FOR CREATIVE COMMUNICATION

While the lecture or sermon or "talk" method may be the most common means of communicating truth in today's typical church setting, it is certainly not the only means. Nor is it, in many cases, the most effective. Do you know why? Consider these facts:

- Many youth workers who passionately desire to communicate truth do not possess the gifts necessary to do so in a large-group, "master-teacher," lecture format.
- Any routine can soon degenerate into the realm of the boring.
- Different approaches to teaching challenge and stimulate different types of students.
- "Preaching" in the traditional sense may be totally inappropriate in a small-group setting.
- Talks most often rob the student of any opportunity for discussion or feedback.

I've been around a college classroom long enough to know that 90–95 percent of my lecture has long since been forgotten forty-eight hours after my last syllable has been uttered. An ego-bust to be sure! But facts are facts.

will apply no matter which of these ideas you may employ. These ideas only represent a sampling of creative ways in which to package what you have studied through the week.

1. Agree-Disagree

Would you like to polarize your group while eliciting electrically charged comments? When touching upon a controversial subject, why not create a list of statements carefully chosen to generate opposing responses? Allow me to introduce you to the agree-disagree sheet.

Divide the room in half. Hang an "agree" sign on one wall, a "disagree" sign on the other. Hand each student the list. After they have marked each statement "agree" or "disagree," read one statement and instruct the students to move to the corresponding side of the room. Let them have at it. Allow five minutes for the members of each side to try to persuade those on the other side to cross over. Then move to a second statement and try it again. Prepare yourself for some heated debate. Once the students have exhausted all their arguments, the stage will be set for you to tell them what God says about each statement. A golden teaching opportunity will have been created.

2. Role play

When teaching from a narrative passage of Scripture, rather than verbally describing the scene, why not have the students re-create the scene? Ask for a group of volunteers or select some students yourself. Your challenge to this improvised drama ensemble? "Take us there. Cause us to visualize how the scene might have appeared."

Lazarus has died. How do Mary and Martha feel? Have two girls volunteer to "become" Mary and Martha and show us how they might have reacted to his death. Don't just tell us that Jesus wept; let us watch our Lord emotionally break at the loss of His friend, and then see His power as He calmly takes control and calls Lazarus out of the tomb.

Create a typical teenage situation. Set up the scenario. For example, on the Sunday morning after summer camp, create this scene: "At camp, a student decided that he needed to change his attitude toward his parents. But the minute he got home, his parents jumped on his case. His mountaintop high crashed and burned on his own living-room floor." Believe me, this story can be retold a thousand times. Many of your students will experience immediate identification. Two students will play the role of the parents. One will play an antagonistic older brother. One will be the camper. Watch and listen to your students as they relate to you how they might respond in the same circumstances. Allow them to share with the others what in fact did happen when they got home from camp. Discuss together the biblical principles that should be obeyed, the reasons behind them, and the difficulties in implementing them in real-life situations.

3. Field trips

The best learning may not take place within the four walls of the junior high room at church. There exists a whole world of "class-

A FIELD TRIP ON COMPASSION

Randy Strickland, one of my former students, wanted to teach his junior high youth group about the plight of the homeless in his city. He created an event. His students met in the church parking lot on a Friday night. Randy provided each one with one cardboard box and one can of beans and tuna. He drove them to a park in the city, and that's where they spent the night. Naturally, Randy informed the parents ahead of time and adequate adult leadership accompanied the students. The editor of the local newspaper got wind of the trip and dispatched a reporter to cover the story. The young people sat spellbound as one homeless man told the students, "Don't do drugs. Do you want to spend the rest of your life sleeping on park benches like me? This is what drugs will do to you. Don't do drugs." Then Randy led in a brief Bible study concerning Christ's compassion for the "harassed and helpless" (Matthew 9:36, NIV). Believe me, you will never generate that kind of learning experience in a classroom.

rooms" in which life-changing teaching can take place.

In one of my classes at the college, a number of students asked me about runaways and prostitutes. They had no clue as to what these people looked like or how they acted. In response, I set up a mystery trip.

The entire class boarded some vans and we proceeded south on the Golden State Freeway. The students just knew we were headed to Hollywood Boulevard to see some hookers. They were wrong. We ended up in the parking lot of the county morgue and were escorted in by a sheriff friend of mine. My students' introduction to the morgue went something like this: "You wanted to see some runaways and prostitutes, right? Well, I decided to show you where most of them end up. You do not have to go beyond these doors if you don't want to. But if you do, you will not come out the same." Needless to say, peer pressure being what it is, everyone went in.

We saw sights the general public never sees—autopsy rooms,

body bags, decomposed flesh. We smelled the stench of decay. The kicker came when our guide ushered us into a refrigerated room containing twenty-four teenagers, their bodies stacked three high around the perimeter of the room. Each person there had died within the last seventy-two hours. "You can tell the runaways," the coroner told us. "When we do the autopsy, their lungs show no signs of air pollution like they would if they lived here in Los Angeles." While I thought my students' lives would change as a result of that trip, I'll tell you what: I'll never be the same again.

4. Learner involvement projects

Revelation 16 ought to strike terror in the heart of everyone who reads the horrifying account of the bowls of God's wrath. Can we make John's predictions come alive? How about turning the class into a group of news reporters? Some will write an eyewitness account for the morning paper. Others will conduct television interviews of those experiencing firsthand the dreaded disasters. A select few can represent political figures attempting to calm the American people in the face of worldwide destruction. How about one or two acting like liberal preachers trying to explain the mysterious disappearance of millions of people and the devastation of countless others? Still others could write letters home reflecting the desperation they might feel at not knowing the conditions of those they love.

Would you like your students to appreciate in a new way the freedom of worship we enjoy in this country? Create an "Underground Night." Determine a secret rendezvous in which you will hold your next Bible study. Hand out a coded message revealing the whereabouts of the study. Inform them that they must sneak in unseen, arriving at differing times so as to not attract attention. Arrange to have some adults, dressed as state police, break up the meeting and drag off the leaders.

5. Bible baseball

This works great when you sense a need to have your young people review a large amount of information they have recently been taught. Divide the class into two teams. Assign both teams the same chapter for a ten-minute personal study. Develop a series of questions based on the passage. On index cards write the words *single, double, triple,* or *home run.* A student will draw from this stack of cards. Ask the student one of your questions. If his card reads *double,* a correct answer will result in a runner on second base; a wrong answer results in an out. Each base runner will advance the same number of bases as the batter (for example, a runner on third can score on a single). Allow three outs per inning and play as many innings as time will allow. You can easily adapt the rules to fit virtually any team sport.

6. Media

Play a contemporary song and evaluate the lyrics from a biblical perspective. Point out the emptiness, confusion, deception, or despair communicated by the words. Show a video clip and discuss its message.

Pass out current newspapers and magazines. After a brief discussion of a biblical truth, have the students find contemporary news events that illustrate the truth you have just articulated.

The use of a medium can be as simple or elaborate as you would like. Do you have any students or staff members who enjoy taking pictures? If so, challenge them to put together a slide-tape presentation on a given topic, utilizing music, scenes from their schools, student interviews, etc. I can guarantee that you will have no problem getting teenagers to respond to a video camera or a microphone. In terms of impact, nothing will ever eclipse the potency of students talking to students about their own guilt, pain, loneliness, or search for the truth.

7. Question-and-answer session

This is my favorite means of communication. Several times each year I will set aside a day to sit on a stool, Bible in hand, and allow the students to ask me anything they want about the Bible, the Christian life, their lives or mine.

According to Acts 17:2, Paul "reasoned with them from the Scriptures." Our word *dialogued* comes from the word translated *reasoned. Dieleksato* literally means "to teach with the method of question and answer."* Paul used a give-and-take dialogue approach

*Rienecker, Fritz. *Linguistic Key to the Greek New Testament.* Grand Rapids: Zondervan, 1980, page 305.

in his teaching. You might consider this approach yourself.

I'll tell you why I so greatly enjoy this method. By taking the questions from the floor, I can (1) stay sharp in my own understanding of the Bible, (2) address the issues most vital in the thinking of my students, (3) validate my credibility as a teacher when I answer questions "on the spot," (4) enjoy a two-way interaction with my students, and (5) vividly demonstrate that the Bible does indeed have the answers for every conceivable need of the human heart.

8. Panel discussions

State a subject, bring in two or three "experts," preferably those who hold to slightly differing views, and emcee a talk-show style discussion. The topics abound: abortion, AIDS, the draft, suicide, materialism, evolution, women's rights, racism, etc. Play the devil's advocate. Put some people on the spot. Force your students to think through some tough issues. Controversy sometimes spawns the most teachable settings in the lives of our teenagers. Capitalize on these opportunities.

9. Case studies

Case studies might come under the *Reader's Digest* designation, "Drama in Real Life." They are true stories in which certain individuals face major decisions. The stories should be given in an open-ended format, leaving the solutions in the hands of the students. "What should Cathy do in this situation and why?" When writing your case study, make certain the identity of the individual remains anonymous. Write out key discussion questions and a scriptural guide to aid the students as they formulate their conclusions.

Can you imagine the discussion true-to-life case studies would produce? Get the staff together and brainstorm some zingers.

10. Chalk talk

If you have any artistic flare at all, this one's for you! Have you ever watched someone paint or draw a picture? Our own innate curiosity holds us captive to the canvas. While drawing your masterpiece, relate a biblical principle through personal testimony or storytelling. At the conclusion of your story, put the finishing touches on your drawing, and watch the excitement flash on the faces of your stu-

CASE STUDY: TEEN PREGNANCY

Wendy just celebrated her fourteenth birthday with an unexpected and shocking discovery: she is pregnant. She told her boyfriend and he responded, "Oh no." She hasn't heard from him since. Her parents have not been told. Since her dad serves as a deacon in her church, he would never understand. If she has the baby, she will have to drop out of school; the embarrassment would be overwhelming. Every one of her friends has urged her to have an abortion. She wishes the baby would just die. That would be the easiest. She even punched herself in the stomach, hoping to cause a miscarriage. Sometimes Wendy wishes her own life would end. She finally breaks down and tells you the whole story, hoping that you can somehow wave a magic wand and make everything all right. Picture Wendy sitting across from you, very much a child at fourteen, facing a very adult situation. How would you respond?

dents as your picture perfectly ties your whole message together.

I once watched in rapt amazement as one artist covered his canvas with blue and orange smudges. By relating events in his own life, he took a piece of chalk and drew five thick black vertical lines across his picture. Everyone moaned as we watched him virtually ruin his creation. "But God's power will always be perfected in our weakness." As he communicated his thoughts, we saw black lines being transformed into trees, blue smudges become a lake, and orange hues soften into a sunrise. "The canvas represents our lives, the artist is none other than the God of the universe, the chalk corresponding to the events in our lives, all working to bring beauty out of ashes." A more powerful message can never be preached!

These are but ten examples of creative Bible teaching. We are limited only by our creativity. If variety is indeed the spice of life, think through a list of your own. And if you try something and it fails, so what? Go back to the drawing board and try again. If your students know you love them, love can cover a multitude of sins, even including a bad lesson once in a while!

CASE STUDY: DIVORCE

For several months now George's parents have been struggling. That's really putting it mildly; they have been having knock-down-drag-out fights. Last night, George's mother sat him down and admitted to him the thing he feared the most: "Your father and I have filed for divorce." Now both parents want custody and George must decide with whom he wants to live. In an attempt to win his love and loyalty, both his mom and dad continue to sow seeds of disloyalty toward the other. They have decided on only one fact: the house will be sold and both will move out of town (memories, you know). Uncertainty characterizes George's future. He may have to leave all of his friends and completely start over. There may be severe financial pressures as well. His thoughts about the future nearly scare him to death.

Out of desperation, he comes by and asks for some helpful advice. What will you say to him?

CHECKING YOUR HEART:
A Personal EKG

1. Before determining a teaching method, the effective teacher must first determine his or her teaching schedule. Some methods simply do not lend themselves to every subject. If you have not done so already, sketch out on paper your teaching program for the next three months.

2. As you look over your list of subjects, ask yourself, "How can I best communicate biblical truth concerning these issues? Which method of teaching will prove the most effective?" Obviously, "practice makes perfect." The more experience you have under your belt, the easier this determination will become. Why not review the ten ideas listed in this chapter and select two or three you might try in the next three months? Experiment and evaluate. Ask your students for their evaluation.

3. Put your heads together as a staff and brainstorm your own ideas. Once again, begin with the subject and move to the method. Our topics must be selected based on the needs within our groups, not on the methods we want to employ in teaching.

4. Do you know of other youth workers in your city or denomination? Why not call two or three of them right now and set up a round-table discussion centered on effective teaching techniques? One valuable idea will be well worth the effort.

5. Expose yourself to skilled teachers and determine their most effective methods. Keep your eyes open for effective communication formats. Watch a gifted interviewer at work. Evaluate a variety of news formats, discussion-oriented programming, etc. Make a record of anything that captures your attention as an effective communication strategy and use it.

6. Read. A number of books dealing with the subject of teaching have been included in Appendix J for your enjoyment. Give yourself to the process. You will find that during the upcoming months, you will begin to settle on your most effective methods as you build an ever-increasing file of teaching ideas. At the very beginning of this discussion, we pointed out that teaching is indeed an art. Any art will take time and a concerted effort to develop. Don't shrink from the process; enjoy it!

5

"I Know My Own"
Maintaining a Heart for Understanding the Flock

"I am the good shepherd; and I know My own" (John 10:14).

"And seeing the multitudes, He felt compassion for them, because they were distressed and downcast like sheep without a shepherd" (Matthew 9:36).

Our students are living in perilous times. All of them are facing challenges today that are unprecedented. Four recent movements of culture have coalesced of late to present to youth workers both enormous challenges and exhilarating opportunities. Let's begin our discussion of these movements by taking a brief stroll together down memory lane.

It wasn't too long ago that a God-consciousness dominated the thinking in our land. The founding fathers of our nation deemed it to be so. When they met together some two hundred twenty years ago, they clearly desired for our godly heritage to be passed down from parent to child. Consider the following:

- The documents upon which our nation rests make clear references to "our Creator" and our constitutional guarantee that the government shall not in any way interfere with, nor inhibit, our right to worship whomever we want, whenever we want, and however we want.
- The hymns of our land reflect an America upon which "God shed His grace," a country within which "His Truth is marching on."
- They stamped on their money their lasting legacy: "In God We Trust."
- Many students learned how to read by using the English Bible as their primary textbook.
- Theoretically, every schoolchild every day of his or her life pledges allegiance to our "one nation under God."

My, how times have changed. Copies of the Ten Commandments have been replaced with multi-colored condom posters. What has happened? And how will these changes affect your ministry and mine?

ENORMOUS CHALLENGES

Take a look around you and I am quite confident that you will instantly discern four specific and dramatic trends that are now firmly in place as far as contemporary youth culture is concerned. Each of these four movements could properly begin with the words, "For the first time in our nation's history. . . ."

1. An entire generation of young people has become totally secularized.

Over the past thirty to forty years, God's influence has been subtly, systematically, and strategically removed from the thinking of today's young people. Every last vestige of a "God-breathed" biblical morality is fast evaporating into thin air. Admittedly, I am loathe to recite recent examples since they will become outdated by the time you read this chapter. For the sake of illustration, however, I will offer two.

At the time of this writing, our nation has just concluded its participation in the "Cairo Conference." We attempted to influence the nations of the world to relax their prohibitions against abortion as a modern-day technique to stabilize population growth as we enter the twenty-first century. A bizarre combination of two strange bedfellows blocked our efforts—the Vatican, and the coalition of Islamic Fundamentalists nations. Who would have thought?

Two weeks later, we were greeted with the news that our government now officially approves of embryo experimentation, to be funded with taxpayers' dollars, including the creation of embryos for testing purposes. Hitler would be proud.

Where was the shock and nationwide outrage over these latest examples of our national obsession to traffic in human flesh? By the time you read this, these two examples will be passé. Ask yourself, "What equally horrifying scandals have hit the airwaves in recent days?" Believe me, you won't have to look very far to find them.

How have our students been affected by this acceleration into the moral abyss? I recently overheard two junior highers in Taco Bell talking about their sexual encounters of the past weekend. Ten years ago, I would have addressed such behavior as typical teenage rebellion. Not today. These students are not rebelling. They are living in absolute *obedience* to the moral ethic that they have been taught is right.

Planned Parenthood comes into their classes and passes the prophylactics around the room as if they are the latest gadgets to hit the shelves at *Toys "R" Us*. Students are told where to obtain them and how to use them. Our nation has seared its collective conscience.

Do you understand the impact of all of this? God's influence has been removed from the thinking of today's young people. When we stand before a cross-section of our teenage society, we cannot even begin with Genesis 1:1. We've got to get more basic than that.

2. An entire generation of young people has become totally traumatized.

Horror stories abound. I hear things today that I never anticipated when I began my ministry a mere two decades ago.

Let me share with you the latest addition to my rapidly expanding collection of youthful correspondence. A junior high girl slapped this note into my hand just as she was getting on the church bus for the ride home from camp. She wrote:

> This week you have been such an encouragement to me. You have been the father I've always wanted to have. Thank you for your talk on forgiveness. These are the things I'm forgiving my father for: hitting me for no reason; insulting me; saying mean, cruel, biting things to me; slapping my face in anger; always screaming at me; breaking promises; beating me; lying to me; ignoring me; not listening to me; getting drunk; coming late to pick me up; laughing at me; breaking my toys, my heart, my skin; throwing stuff at me; saying "You make me sick." Thank you for helping me.
> Signed, The Girl in the Third Row

You might be thinking that there's no way these things could be true. "She's just looking for attention," you might be saying under your breath. Admittedly, I have no way of knowing if any or all of these things are true or false. Does it really matter? Anyone so desperate for attention that he or she would cry out in this way must have deep hurt and anguish burning on the inside. The level of pain that I have encountered out there cannot be measured.

As I travel around the countryside, I have found such deep-seated feelings of resentment and bitterness reaching near-epidemic proportions. My book, *Secret Wounds and Silent Cries,* based upon my own embittered past involving my abusive father, has brought hope to scores of kids who can readily relate to the emotional scars that cut deep into my soul.

Just last week a youth pastor brought several of his "best kids" to a recording studio for the purpose of taping a teacher training cassette for Scripture Press. Mind you, this was the cream of his evangelical crop. By the time the two-hour taping was over, the producer came out with two bloodshot eyes and one tear-soaked handkerchief. She was utterly unprepared for the avalanche of gut-wrenching emotions that came crashing in upon her.

The level of trauma to which students today are subjected has radically changed my own preaching style. I used to speak to them with an index finger pointed at their noses. Playing the ever appealing role of the prophet, I happily got in their faces and brought to them a good hefty dose of the fear of God. Not any more. Today, I speak as a broken man to broken students. The pointing index finger has been replaced with two arms of love and warm embrace.

3. An entire generation of young people has lost its sense of "cause."

Do you ever feel a twinge of envy when you look into the faces of today's young people? I surely do. While most adults are locked into their careers, family and financial obligations, and lifestyles, our students know no such restrictions on their futures. They possess the capacity and the opportunity to dream a dream and see a vision. They can set a goal and become virtually anything their little ol' hearts desire. And yet, with a whole world of adventures lying just outside their bedroom windows, most students today are bored. Whenever I tell them that I could wish for five lifetimes to experience the many adventures that I can only think about now, they look at me as if I'd just arrived from Mars. How can this be?

Would I be overly presumptuous to suggest that my generation was the last in our country to have what I like to call a sense of "cause"? Growing up during the 1960s—that turbulent, yet exuberant decade our students read about in their ancient U.S. History textbooks—my generation had a reason to get out of bed in the morning. We knew what life was all about. We had a cause to live for, and if need be, something to die for.

We lived through the Cuban Missile Crisis during which our world was pushed to the brink of nuclear holocaust. We agonized over the assassinations of our leaders. While living in a nation that was divided by the war in Vietnam and the color of a person's skin, we became absolutely convinced that we could burn it all down and create a utopia in its place, securing it firmly upon a tripod of peace, love, and rock and roll.

Free speech became our medium, Berkeley our pulpit, and four mop tops from Liverpool our chief spokesmen. We began the decade by singing simple songs of love as we chanted "She loves you, yeah, yeah, yeah," only to graduate to those words that were destined to become our banner cry, "Give Peace a Chance." We gave the world a concentrated dosage of our witch's brew of free love and LSD at an event forever immortalized as "Woodstock," only to have our efforts go up in smoke that emanated from the barrels of the guns fired on the campus of Kent State University.

The Sixties' generation has sired the generation of the nineties, "Generation X" as some would have it known. While stereotypes are rarely fair, it can be said that most young people today are disillusioned, cynical, apathetic, and bored.

We took to the streets; they sit in parking lots. We carried banners and had our sit-ins; they carry weapons to school and just stand around. We were out to change the world; they have concluded that the world cannot be changed. Our music redefined the medium; their music is written in a minor key. We were out to control our destiny; they have no sense of "tomorrow." As a bumper sticker I read recently so eloquently states, "Life stinks, and then you die."

That's why we in youth work today do err, significantly so, when we fail to challenge our students to take up Christ's cause. Jesus never watered down His challenge; He never sugar-coated His message. He told the crowds up front what He demanded of those who dared to follow Him. "Deny yourselves," Jesus said on more than one occasion. In other words, He exhorted His followers to forget about what *they* wanted, and to align themselves wholeheartedly behind what *He* wanted.

"Take up your cross daily," He continued. He made the issues crystal clear. The multitudes knew exactly what He meant; they saw crosses every day. "Be prepared to die for Me," He was saying, because many of them had to do just that.

"Once you have laid your plans, passions, and ambitions aside in deference to Mine, and once you have accepted the notion that you might one day die for Me, only then can you follow Me." No wonder the crowds went home amazed. No wonder they asked, "Who is this guy?"

If you will permit one reporter's opinion here, I dare say that we may have failed this generation of young people at this point. Is it possible that we have yet to present to them a Jesus worth living for, and if need be, worth dying for? They need to know, indeed they *want* to know, that Jesus is not some ancient and impotent, wishy washy, wacko cult leader who wants to be their buddy. He is the Master of the Universe who wants to be their Lord. When we present Him thus, I believe that they will rally to His side.

4. An entire generation of young people has lost its ability to think critically.

Up until thirty years ago, the dominant medium of communication in our world was the printed page. People grew up reading to one another. Even when they turned on a radio for their nightly entertainment, they listened to people reading to them.

Print, by its very nature, is a static medium. It is fixed and does not change. This paragraph will read tomorrow exactly as it reads today.

Print thus becomes the ideal basis for research, dialogue, analysis, debate, and discussion. The reader can trace the logic or illogic of the writer's arguments. One idea can be built upon another in a progression of thought that leads the reader to a climax and conclusion. Print by its very nature forces its readers to think critically.

Today, the dominant medium of communication is not print, but video. If you don't believe that, then ask your students next Sunday to tell you how many videos, movies, and television shows they watched last week, compared to how many books they read. Indeed, in some quarters, not only do young people not read, but if the truth be known, far too many of them can't read.

Video is the antithesis of print. Video is a dynamic medium that changes constantly. One image after another, in full color, complete with Dolby stereo sound, bombards our minds at a dizzying pace. Video can be used to elicit virtually any human emotion the person behind the camera desires, from hilarity to horror.

The upshot of this is a rather troublesome fact of life. For the first time in our nation's history, we have a generation of young people on our hands which is ripe for the picking where emotional manipulation is concerned. Rather than knowing how to think critically, they only know how to react emotionally. They are sitting ducks for someone to come along with a slick presentation complete with tear-jerking stories and manipulate them to do whatever he or she wants for personal profit. And as you well know, there are plenty of vultures out there just waiting to feast upon their unsuspecting carcasses.

EXHILARATING OPPORTUNITIES

So what do we do in light of these ominous characteristics? Should we start popping Prozac to head off some impending depression that could easily settle over us like a fog of despair? No way. We've been handed a golden opportunity to make a difference like never before. Nature abhors a vacuum. You and I have the answers that can fill this hopeless void.

As a personal note of encouragement to you, let me just say that I have just come off of the best summer of youth camp and conference speaking that I have ever had. I found the students as a whole to be hungrier, friendlier, more open, appreciative, and *more responsive* than at any other time in my twenty years of so of youth speaking. My mail affirms the fact that even though they have been burned, many of them badly, young people today are ready and willing to turn their ears toward someone they are confident will love them and will tell them the truth. This generation is at a crossroads; we can seize the moment!

Allow me to suggest several ministry principles that we might observe in light of the portrait I have just painted regarding youth culture today.

1. Since our kids are secularized, we must make the teaching of the Word of God the centerpiece of our youth ministries.

Far too many youth workers are dying out there because they are trying to run a three-ring circus. Somewhere they have become influenced by the false notion that kids want a whole menu of monthly activities thrown their way. This could not be farther from the truth.

First of all, when we surrendered to the Lord as far as ministry was concerned, we didn't anticipate that we'd be running a sanctified YMCA. We were not called by Christ to be ringmasters for Barnum and Bailey. We are ministers. Armed with the Bible, we have answers that no one else can provide. If our students do not hear the truth from us, then to whom can they turn?

Second, if we give the bulk of our time to pulling off ski trips and winter camps, we'll burn out in a second. We cannot begin to penetrate a campus, counsel needy students, influence faculty members and administrators, lead effective Bible studies, and fill the empty hours of every student in our group by providing them with endless activities, only to become frustrated that more kids don't come. If the pressure to fill a calendar comes primarily from the church board or parents, then skillful diplomacy will have to be enacted as we explain to them where the priorities of our ministries lie.

Third, we should encourage our students to be active—on their junior high, middle school, or high school campuses. How else can they exert a godly influence at school? A healthy percentage of a school's ASB officers, cheerleaders, athletes, musicians, drama team members, club members, etc. should come from the ranks of our young people. As this happens, we can begin to influence the school from the inside out. This cannot happen if we expect our students to spend time with their families (those who have them), do their homework with a commitment toward excellence (how can they positively influence their teachers if they don't?), give of their time voluntarily at school, and then faithfully attend all of our activities. Something has to give.

Please do not take the above comments to an extreme that I do not intend. Surely there is a place for activities. (Chapter 11 is devoted entirely to the effective planning and execution of activities.) But never at the expense of our teaching. Students will elevate their attendance at our Bible studies to places of personal priority only when we place a premium on our preparation and delivery of the Truth to our teens.

2. Since our kids are traumatized, we must . . .

• Give praise, not flattery. Flattery focuses upon outward, changeable characteristics, such as girl's hair or a guy's football stats. Flattery will only reinforce low self-esteem. "What if he no longer thinks my hair looks pretty?" they may ask. "What if I break my leg and can no longer play? Will she still like me then?" they may wonder.

Praise establishes a person's worth. Praise targets inward character qualities: faithfulness, compassion, honesty, diligence, a willingness to serve, and so on. These are the kinds of qualities that we want to build up and reinforce.

• Never make fun of a young person in any way. I recently watched in horror as a youth pastor proceeded to verbally assassinate three first-time visitors to a youth group of 150 people. He was trying to be funny, but he got his laughs at someone else's expense.

Many of our students have fragile emotions when it comes to their opinions of themselves. Effective youth workers recognize this and choose their remarks accordingly.

• Become transparent and vulnerable. Nothing will break down barriers faster, and build respect quicker, than if you and I choose to be real. Young people today, like never before, are desperately searching for someone who is authentic. They need to know that we struggle and fail just like them. We are in this battle together, with them in the trenches. We have good days and we have our fair share of bad days. We know it to be true; they need to know it too.

- Be patient. Some young people can drive the best of youth workers to distraction. As one buddy of mine recently relented, "I love to see them come, but I love to see them go." Understandably so. But let us never forget what they may be going home to. Many, if not most, of our students go home to a war zone. They need our compassion, understanding, acceptance, and love.
- Follow through on our commitments. We cannot afford to join the ranks of those who have betrayed our students. They need someone they can count on; we should be at the top of their lists.

3. Since our kids have lost their sense of cause, we must mobilize them into a mighty army of good soldiers.

A youth group needs a clearly defined reason that it exists. Our teens ought to know why they are here. Like skilled military officers, the responsibility resides within us to mobilize our students into a spiritual squadron ready to assault the principalities and powers that hold this generation in a blinding bondage.

Our worship services should be equipping services. Week by week our students can receive the truth they need to lead victoriously fulfilling lives, and the tools they need to help others experience the same. This is Ephesians 4 in action. Our students should understand that they are not going to school primarily as students, but as commandos sent on an eternal rescue mission with the souls of their friends hanging in the balance.

I'll tell you this from my own personal experience: There is nothing more electrifying than to be in the presence of a group of turned on and fired up young people. The fire in their eyes and the boundless energy with which they face life are both infectious and inspiring. While it may take much time and effort to get them to this place, the results are well worth the efforts.

4. Since our kids have lost their ability to think critically, we must reinforce in them both what we believe and why we believe it.

Ours is a rational faith. There are reasons why God has said what He has. Our students need to know what those reasons are.

Not long ago, on a television talk show, four mothers who had sold their babies at birth were reunited with their now grown children. Sparks were flying around the studio as each mother tried to explain to her abandoned child why she made the choice she did. Tears of anger and rage flowed freely as each child cursed his or her mom for turning her back on her child. This sorry sight was exploitation and sensationalism at its worst.

In the course of things, one woman grabbed the microphone from the host and shouted at the moms in an uncontrolled explosion of pent-up emotion, "Why didn't you just abort them? Why put them through this?" Imagine for a moment that you are a sixteen-year-old girl and you just found out that you're pregnant. Your friends, *Planned Parenthood,* et al., are telling you to get an abortion. You're just not sure. And then you watch this display. What choice would you make?

It is no longer enough for us to tell our students, "Thou shalt not. . . . " We must tell them *why.* They must be trained to think critically about such complex life-and-death issues, even if it means we must start at square one. Such is our challenge and our privilege.

These are great days. We have been handpicked by God to be parachuted into the midst of "the good fight" (1 Timothy 1:18). Eternal destinies are at stake. We have been called by our Lord to do something significant. What we do matters. We dare not shrink from the task. Rather, let's seize the day and exploit our God-given opportunities to the full, for our students' good and Christ's glory.

CHECKING YOUR HEART:
A Personal EKG

1. Romans 1:18-32 describes the process by which a society becomes secularized. Study the passage and isolate those principles that led to this reality in our own nation. Pass on what you learn to the young people you teach.

2. How can you visualize achievement in your young people? Can you creatively reinforce in their minds their value to you and to God? For example, one of the girls in my group was cut from her volleyball team. She felt devastated. I purposely selected her to form with me a two-person volleyball team, and together we challenged everyone in the group. You can't begin to imagine what a lift that was to her; she'll never forget it. Can you identify those in your group who need a similar "lift" from you? You may be the only source of affirmation that they have.

3. Plan a weekend retreat for your incoming junior high or middle school students. The purpose of this retreat can be twofold: (1) to welcome them into the youth group; and (2) to prepare them for the many challenges that they are going to experience. Affirm to them that you will walk with them through this transitional period of their lives. Many of the aspects of youth culture described in this chapter could become the basis for your teaching ministry at this retreat.

4. Every student in your youth group has been skillfully created by God (Psalm 139) and chosen by Him to exert a godly influence in an ungodly world (Matthew 5:13-14). Think of some creative ways your students can begin to exert a godly influence in their world.

5. Formulate a list of every conceivable conflict with which teenagers deal: family, friendships, dating, peer pressures, bitterness, etc. Find biblical solutions for each one and allow these to become the basis of your Bible study curriculum. Be sure to include not just what God has said, but why He has said it.

6. Review the four principles listed on pages 69–72. List some practical ways some of these ideas can be implemented in your group. This list is certainly not exhaustive. Can you add other principles that you gleaned from this chapter, or from your own or other youth workers' experiences in working with youth?

7. Do you ever find yourself feeling discouraged about the condition of our world today? Do you ever feel like giving up? If so, you are not alone. We as youth workers are like puny, pipsqueak little Davids trying to take on a society of Goliath proportions. When these overwhelming feelings of inadequacy strike, please remember that one man or one woman plus God equals a majority anywhere. We cannot lose, because we have already won!

6

"Do the Work of an Evangelist" *Maintaining a Heart for Cultural Penetration*

"Do the work of an evangelist" (2 Timothy 4:5).

"For they themselves report about us what kind of a reception we had with you, and how you turned to God from idols to serve a living and true God, and to wait for His Son from heaven, whom He raised from the dead, that is Jesus, who delivers us from the wrath to come" (1 Thessalonians 1:9-10).

The Tribulation had finally ended. The Millennium was about to begin. At least that's how I felt. It had been four years of college and three years of seminary by the time I walked across the platform and received that most important piece of parchment. Seven years of exams, papers, assignments, projects, reports, speeches, and lectures were over. Graduation day came on a Saturday. My first day as a full-time, bona fide youth pastor came on Sunday.

The usual fuss and feathers that accompany the beginning of any new endeavor filled the air. I was introduced as the new youth pastor, the crowds applauded, and the young people responded with a party. I was loving life—for a while. Monday morning came too quickly.

This particular Monday was an exceptionally beautiful day. The sun was shining, the wind was blowing, and the birds were singing—but I was dying. I am simply not a sit-behind-the-desk kind of guy. The thought of locking myself away within the four walls of an office did not suit my style. I began to wonder, "Have I spent the last seven years of my life preparing for this? Is this what youth ministry is all about? Is this how a city filled with teenagers is reached? Is this what cultural penetration is all about?" Confusion and discouragement began to creep in on me like a fog.

For years I had been chomping at the bit. I couldn't wait to get out and get started. I saw the young people all around me as desperately needy, and I had the answers. The goal of penetrating their culture by learning their language, feeling their heartbeat, pinpointing their struggles, and influencing their world was exhilarating. My heart burned with a passion to penetrate the teenagers' world, becoming a dominant influence over what they believed and how they lived.

Jesus commanded cultural penetration: "Go into all the world and preach the gospel to all creation" (Mark 16:15). The troublesome question becomes "Where and how do we begin?" Sitting within my four walls on that beautiful Monday morning, the answer suddenly dawned on me. Cultural penetration takes place when we penetrate the school campuses in our areas.

THE CAMPUS AS A MISSION FIELD

My thoughts built one on another something like this: Within the vast panorama of everything we would consider to be a part of youth culture, the teenager visits one place, at least theoretically, every day—his school campus. The school has replaced the family as the most influential dimension of his life. At school, the young person receives his education, builds friendships, begins to date, formulates most of his values, encounters peer pressure, makes life-determining choices, pursues a sport or hobby, and spends the bulk of his time.

As I thought this through, the clouds of confusion and discouragement suddenly lifted. I got up from my desk and told my secretary, "I'm going back to school!"

Ah, ignorance is bliss. No one told me campus penetration couldn't be done. No one ever mentioned "the separation of church and state" or the ACLU. So off I went, naively to be sure. Campus conquest had begun.

Did it work? Can a public junior high or high school campus actually be penetrated?

- Fact: My staff and I walked into the bleachers during a football game, and virtually everyone in the house knew exactly who we were and what we stood for.
- Fact: I was able to walk onto the campuses any time I wanted with no resistance whatsoever.
- Fact: I gained permission to sit in a variety of classes, hearing for myself the same information the young people were hearing.
- Fact: The entire drama department at one high school was called into the principal's office and threatened with the mandatory censoring of a play if they did not clean it up themselves. The cast revolted, screaming at the top of their lungs, "Freedom of speech! Freedom of speech!" After a forty-five-minute impasse, the vice principal asked this question: "Dewey was here for opening night. Now what do you think?" The room became deathly silent, and the play was voluntarily censored.
- Fact: A gay teacher openly encouraged his students to accept homosexuality as an alternative lifestyle. I took him out to dinner and expressed to him my horror at the thought of twisting the moral fabric of these young and impressionable students. In response, he challenged me to a school-wide debate on the subject. He lost the debate, and biblical morality became the topic of discussion on that campus for weeks to come.
- Fact: The teachers went on strike. Every student in the place

headed for the beach while the young people in my youth group went to class. In response, the principal personally called me to thank me for the positive influence I was having on his campus.

• Fact: A girl on the softball team became ill and, within two weeks, died. The student body was stunned. I was asked to participate at the funeral, a golden opportunity to share the Gospel with 80 percent of the student body.

PRINCIPLES FOR CAMPUS PENETRATION

How can the penetration of a campus become a reality? What about the separation of church and state? Aren't there principles that will work in one area but may not work in another? Campus conquest is a possibility no matter where you live. If you follow the principles laid out in this chapter, your presence on campus will become a reality, guaranteed!

1. Pray the prayer of John Knox.

His famous prayer has echoed throughout the hallowed halls of church history for decades: "Give me Scotland or I die." Influence comes only as a result of a burning heart. God answered Knox's prayer by allowing his voice to be the dominant influence in all of Scotland.

"Lord, give me Burroughs High School or else I will die." Burroughs High School boasted a student body of 1,500. I routinely walked around the perimeter and through the campus of Burroughs High as well as each of the other schools in my immediate area of influence. I prayed specifically that God would give them to me. "God, as I stand for Your truth, allow my voice to become the dominant influence at this school."

This prayer follows our Lord's instructions to His disciples concerning the proper pattern for prayer. In what has come to be called the Lord's Prayer, Jesus told His disciples to pray, "Hallowed be Thy name" (Matthew 6:9). Literally translated, this request should read, "Set Your name apart as holy."

Every youth worker ought to passionately desire to see the name of Jesus Christ set apart as holy at every school our young people attend. The blasphemy of His name and the mockery of His standards take place every day on campus. "The effective prayer of a righteous man can accomplish much" (James 5:16). Praying in this way directly assaults the kingdom of darkness. Satan has had undisputed control of our junior high and high school campuses far too long. As you participate in regular and fervent prayer for each school, be prepared for a fight. The enemy doesn't relinquish turf easily.

2. Create legitimate, nonthreatening reasons to be on campus.

The importance of this principle cannot be overstated. We nail our coffins shut the moment we walk into the principal's office asking for his permission to come on campus. Those for whom this tactic has worked are the exception, never the rule. Ninety-nine times out of one hundred the well-intentioned principal will cite "the separation of church and state" as he escorts us off the grounds.

Frankly, I thank God every day for the so-called "separation of church and state." While we can argue all day long about the constitutionality of our on-campus rights, the "separation of church and state" keeps members of every cult, neo-Nazi group, and so on, off the campuses. If the schools grant permission for us to come on campus, they must grant permission to anyone who asks. Our students are victimized enough. The "separation of church and state" offers the only protection our young people have from those who would exploit them for their own hellish ends.

Campus penetration has been achieved when we become recognized as a natural part of the surroundings. By utilizing a legitimate reason to enter the campus, we create the perception in the minds of students and administration alike that we belong there. Our presence on campus ought to be seen as natural as any tree or building in the place. This can be accomplished only as we hang around the school in a legitimate and, therefore, nonthreatening manner.

Three facts must be understood at this point. First, the legal issues relative to "the separation of church and state" become irrelevant the moment we legitimately walk on campus. Second, the campus penetration process takes time. We must be patient, allowing God to open the right doors at the right time. Third, ours must always be a servant's role. We desire to make our school system the best. We want to become a positive, supportive, and wholesome influence on campus. As we serve and support in any way we can, we earn the right to be heard.

GETTING ON CAMPUS

• Anything open to the general public constitutes a legitimate presence on campus. Evening football and basketball games provide us with open invitations to come on in. Drama productions, band concerts, sports banquets, photo shows, graduations, and open houses provide you with golden opportunities to make your rounds on campus.

• The campus buzzes after school hours. After 3 o'clock, the campus becomes open territory. You can attend girls' softball games, guys' baseball games, basketball practices, swim and track meets, drama rehearsals, etc., to your heart's desire.

• Visit the office for school-related information. You'll certainly want to obtain a schedule of activities, purchase tickets, or inquire about upcoming events. Why not visit the office during the lunch hour? And why not park your car on the opposite side of the campus from the office so that you will have to walk through the campus to get there? Without a doubt, you will want to stop and talk to some students along the way, right?

• Have students invite you to visit a class. This was the method I initially used. It worked like a charm. Most teachers welcome community interest and support. Once the student has obtained permission from the teacher for you to visit the class, requesting a visitor pass from the front desk becomes a mere formality.

• Meet a teacher for lunch. At least one Christian teacher hangs out on most every campus. Most have a desire to see God use them as a positive influence in the students' lives. Most teachers will welcome your support and would cherish an opportunity to discuss the possibilities and build a friendship with someone of like mind and heart.

• Arrange for a student to use you as a project in a photo class. I needed some black-and-white glossies for publicity, and the students needed someone they could "shoot." Fortunately, my students weren't too swift when it came to photography. What should have been a one-day project turned into a week-long marathon. After five class sessions I knew every student in the class and had established an ongoing relationship with several.

• Have someone interview you for the school paper. Not only does this create an opportunity for you to be on campus, but it provides a platform within the school itself from which you can express your views on a given subject.

• Help with election speeches and posters. By offering your assistance as a speech coach you can earn the privilege of being in the auditorium during the election assembly. The school becomes wallpapered with posters during the week prior to the election. The campus transforms itself into a beehive of parents and friends who are lending a helping hand in painting and hanging these posters. You may as well become one of the bees, don't you think?

• Assist during athletic events. Most events require the help of several individuals. Coaches need people who can keep stats, run the clock, work a scoreboard, sell programs, serve at the concession stands, etc. If nothing else, you can offer to stand on the sidelines and take pictures to be used at the athletic banquet. Or why not become a certified assistant coach?

• Become a noon monitor. The local junior high school pays one of my youth ministry students to check for lunch passes during the lunch hour. Every day he talks to every junior higher at the school.

• Try your hand at substitute teaching. Can you imagine supplementing your income while spending time in the classroom itself? If you substitute, you must operate within certain limitations. However, you may respond to any question the student may ask in or out of the classroom.

3. Have the proper goals.

Our presence on campus places us in a strategic position to accomplish some tremendous goals.

We can meet, establish, and deepen relationships with young

people, teachers and administrators. The single most important principle I have ever learned in youth ministry is this: truth flows through relationships.

We can keep our fingers on the pulse beat of each school, affording us unlimited opportunities to influence the school as we earn the right to be heard.

Our teaching ministry will become more effective. Our messages will take on a whole new relevance when we illustrate biblical principles with current school events.

We can be seen as the greatest support the administrators, teachers, and coaches have. Remember, they are not the enemy. They are at worst pawns in the hand of the enemy. Our influence on the schools grows exponentially as we gain an influence over the key people in places of authority. We are seeking to redeem them just as fervently as we are the young people they influence.

We can become the bridge into the youth group. Attendance at a Bible study or social activity must never become a pressure proposition. As young people meet us and begin to open up to us, an invitation to a Bible study becomes a natural. There will be no fear of walking into a foreign environment. A relationship will have already been established.

We will serve as models for our young people, demonstrating right before their eyes how they can build relationships and share their faith with their friends. Most of our young people would be more than willing to share their message if they only knew how. They desperately need examples to follow. We will become their examples.

4. Build genuine relationships.

Young people will eventually open up and share with us on a fairly deep level once a commitment of trust has been established. The common experience linking us human beings together involves a four-letter word: pain. We hurt, they hurt. Openness begets openness.

Many a well-meaning youth worker has committed a grave mistake by creating the perception that he or she has it all together in every area of life. Thinking to gain the respect of the young people, such a leader only creates the illusion of having achieved a level of success the young people feel utterly incapable of reaching.

God's power is expressed through our weakness (2 Corinthians 12:9). By sharing out of the context of our own personal pain, we immediately create a common bond with others who are enduring pain of their own. The walls break down. Their fear of sharing with us disappears. Our willingness to be vulnerable before the young people we meet allows them the same luxury in response to us.

The most effective evangelism takes place when we apply the good news of the Gospel to the specific needs of each young person. We have a God who can meet every need. To those from broken homes He becomes a father to the fatherless (Psalm 68:5). The brokenhearted can read of a Jesus who wept at the tomb of His friend (John 11:35). To the fearful He is the God who holds the future in His hand (Revelation 1:8). To the anxious He offers a peace that passes all understanding (Philippians 4:7). To the guilty He provides forgiveness and cleansing (Isaiah 1:18). No more positive and compelling message exists in the world today than the Gospel of Jesus Christ. Every need of every hurting heart can be met by its truth.

5. View the school as people groups.

Two thousand young people at one school can be an overwhelming and intimidating thought. How do we even begin to reach 2,000 people? The task seems impossible until we visualize the school as people groups.

Every student fits in somewhere. The football team, class officers, cheerleading squad, drama team, band, photo club, tennis team, drug crowd (they hang out on the street just outside the school), and the nonparticipants (these students are generally good kids who come to school, sit in class, and go home to study) all qualify as people groups.

Over the years the Spirit of God will work His way through one or more people groups. The process takes place on both a natural and a supernatural level. Members of the youth staff naturally tend to hang out around areas of personal interest. Those who enjoy baseball will attend the games. The musically inclined will be drawn to the band. As relationships begin to form, the Spirit of God supernaturally uses these contacts as conduits through which the truth can flow.

Defining a school in terms of people groups makes the penetration of a campus a realistic goal. We can consolidate our efforts by narrowing our focus to a few groups rather than hundreds of individuals.

6. Don't give up, even if asked to leave the campus.
This is war. We have to anticipate opposition and reaction. Satan has had unrivaled possession of school campuses for decades. He will not relinquish his hold easily.

After six years of undisputed access to two high school campuses in my city, through no fault of my own, I was asked to leave. Several of my friends told me, "Without campus access, you're through." Were they right?

Let me tell you the outcome:

- One hundred parents spontaneously appealed to the school board for my return to the campuses. Every newspaper picked up the story and without exception took my side, supporting me as a wholesome and positive influence.
- Teachers came out of the woodwork on my behalf. At the teachers' invitation, I lectured in several classes concerning the needs of young people in contemporary society as well as my own personal commitment to Christ.
- The athletic director gave me the permission to involve myself in the athletic program anytime and in any way I chose.
- I was asked to chaperone at the senior prom.
- My picture was taken with the graduating class for placement on the inside front cover of the yearbook.

I gained even greater campus access after being kicked off the campus than I ever dreamed of before that traumatic experience. Before my "removal," life was simple and I took my privileges for granted. Now I was forced to be creative. Creativity resulted in incredible privileges and opportunities to exert a godly influence.

CHECKING YOUR HEART:
A Personal EKG

1. Prayer is the essential priority for campus penetration. List some ways you can creatively involve your young people and staff in concerted prayer for each campus.

You might consider these examples:

a. All-night prayer meetings. Begin with some singing, and then give a challenge concerning personal purity and the need to confess before God anything that would hinder the effectiveness of your prayer. Divide the evening into categories: school administrators, teachers, coaches, members of the drama team, football team, etc. Pray until every school has been thoroughly covered.

b. Morning watch. Meet with interested students one morning per week per school. Extend an invitation to other youth pastors and their students. Meet in a neutral location (a home, business, or restaurant) in close proximity to the campus.

c. Set aside a regular Bible study night for prayer. This should be done at the beginning of each semester. Announce well in advance the purpose of the study. Begin with a short devotional concerning the importance of prayer and focus on the friends and teachers of each of your young people.

d. Brainstorm with your staff every possible legitimate reason you can create for being on campus. My staff has volunteered as teacher assistants, lighting technicians for drama productions, makeup assistants, lunch monitors, etc. We have had staff work as librarians, nurses, student teachers, security, and a whole host of other jobs. Be willing to take a risk. If turned down in one pursuit, come back with another. See it as an adventure. Allow God to open the right doors at the right time.

2. Get a list of every activity and sporting event for the coming year. Which events will you attend? Schedule them now before your calendar fills up. Plan to meet some of your students at designated places the nights of the events. This will communicate your individual concern for your students as well as create an opportunity for you to meet their friends.

3. No doubt someone will say, "When will I ever have time to penetrate one campus, let alone several?" You must set a realistic goal. My desire was to be on each campus once each week. My average stay was one hour. Block the time out on your weekly calendar. I can assure you that any time spent on campus penetration will prove to be an investment guaranteed to pay long-term dividends.

Have you considered combining campus penetration with other responsibilities? Visitation programs can be a constant frustration. Young people rarely stay home. Begin to visit young people at school. When a young person wants to meet for counseling, arrange to meet at school. Set up an over-the-line game with some guys on the field after school. Get up a basketball game and invite students who are walking by to join in the action. Creativity is the key. The sky is the limit when it comes to ideas.

4. Work up a list of general questions you can use to generate a conversation with the young people you meet. General questions can be answered with public information. "What classes are you taking?" is a general question. "Do you have any hobbies?" is a general question. "How much does your mother really weigh?" is not a general question. Work up a list and memorize it so that you will be ready when the opportunity presents itself.

5. Start slowly and don't wear out your welcome. Follow this rule of thumb: the more public the event, the less of a risk you are taking. Begin by attending athletic events. No one will question your presence there. As you gain recognizability, you can take more daring risks (such as sitting in a class). Be sensitive to the administration's response to you. Remember, the privilege of campus visitation must be earned, never demanded.

7

"Having Thus a Fond Affection for You"
Maintaining a Heart for the Personal Touch

"Having thus a fond affection for you, we were well-pleased to impart to you not only the gospel of God but also our own lives, because you had become very dear to us" (1 Thessalonians 2:8).

"It just seemed like you were always too busy with the other kids." This last line of her heart-wrenching letter crushed me. My rationalizations came quickly. "Give me a break. I'm not Superman. I'm only the camp speaker. You were only one of 300 kids at the camp. You can't possibly expect me to give undivided attention to each of you. Don't you understand?" Yet the simple fact remained. A very needy girl, rejected by her own family, received a message from me that left an impression far deeper than any sermon I preached from the platform that week: "I am much to busy for you."

Our society has reduced people to mere statistics. Our world has grown cold, callous, and impersonal. God forbid that such a description will ever characterize our youth ministries.

Effective youth ministry must always be person to person. We commit a cardinal sin when we communicate to a young person that we do not have time for him or her.

As our youth ministries expand, every one of us will face the temptation of subordinating the needs of the individual to the needs of the mass. Understandably so. The pressure on us to increase attendance escalates week by week. Some days it feels as if we live and die according to the stats. Let us never forget, however, that the concept of *ministry* demands a wholehearted commitment to meeting the needs of the individual. Once a young person senses our lack of a personal interest in his or her life, our effectiveness as youth workers will be greatly diminished if not destroyed. We must at all costs maintain the personal touch.

I have had a youth group of 4 and a youth group of 500. My experience has proven that the goal of maintaining the personal touch can be achieved with a minimal time commitment regardless of the size of one's youth group.

Let's define our terms. A "personal touch" takes place every time a youth worker singles out a young person as an individual apart from the mass. Every young person in every youth ministry should be given this "touch" at least once every week.

Maintaining a personal touch can become a fun and thrilling expression of our own creativity. By definition, the personal touch must incorporate some out-of-the-ordinary, unexpected, going-the-extra-mile kinds of contacts. First-time visitor letters and absentee cards do not qualify. Anything printed or photocopied coupled with a mailing label hardly communicates a personal message. While these types of mailings cannot and should not be eliminated, they should never lull us into thinking that we have fulfilled our "personal touch" responsibilities.

COMMUNICATING A PERSONAL TOUCH

Let us consider several possible ways we can effectively communicate a personal touch to the young people within our groups. I do not intend to provide you with an exhaustive list. Such a task would be impossible. Nor do I expect anyone to implement every idea. Such a feat would prove impossible. My goal will be achieved if I am able to prompt your thinking as to the best means of maintaining the personal touch in your particular ministry.

1. Greet every young person at every meeting.

A sincere, friendly greeting affirms the worth and importance of the individual. A student ignored becomes a student rejected. The policy of any youth staff must include this objective: every young person will be greeted during every meeting without exception. A sincere handshake, high five, pat on the back, squeeze of the shoulder, or "It's great to see you" can transform anyone's day.

Eye contact communicates undivided attention. A pause for a response after asking someone "How's it going?" expresses genuine concern. "How did you do on your test?" "How is your mother feeling?" "Are you excited about your track meet tomorrow?" Questions such as these demonstrate commitment to an individual. The entire encounter might take only twenty or thirty seconds, but the response will always be the same: "This person really cares about me."

2. Send an occasional note.

Negative messages bombard our young people every day of their lives. The resulting devastation creates a desperate hunger for any semblance of positive reinforcement. An occasional note can easily and effectively satisfy this need.

Set a realistic goal—perhaps five notes per week. Divide your youth group roster accordingly. The notes should be brief by design. A couple of carefully chosen sentences will allow us to thank a young person for his friendship, identify a character quality he has displayed, or wish him the best day ever. An investment of four or

LAYING THE FOUNDATION

1. Commit the time.

We must accept the fact that maintaining the personal touch requires a commitment of our time. The amount of time will vary depending on (1) the number of young people currently involved in our ministries, including both the core and the fringe young people; (2) the number of staff available to help "share the load"; (3) our own schedules; and (4) how elaborate we want to get in our methodology. Would you like to hear some good news? Many of the ideas suggested in this chapter will require a minimum amount of time!

Consider these thoughts. When we reduce ministry to the basic fundamentals, we are talking about personally touching people. Maintaining the personal touch does not constitute a part of ministry, nor is the personal touch a prerequisite to ministry. Maintaining the personal touch *is* ministry. Don't allow the personal touch to become drudgery. View this as the heart and soul of what we are about.

If you feel overburdened already, and find yourself entering this chapter with a whirlwind of apprehensions ("Oh no! What's he going to ask of me now?"), relax. Let's set a realistic, attainable goal. I will show you ways in which you can, with a time commitment of only thirty minutes per week, personally touch no fewer than six students!

2. Operate from pure motives.

A personal touch must flow out of our heartfelt care and concern for each young person. Insincere motives will always leave pain and disillusionment in their wake. I still bear the scar of a phone call I received several years ago. I was invited by the president of my college-age youth group to a Friday night activity. The realization that he cared about me became overwhelming. But the bubble burst when he said, "We want you to come because we want as big a group out as we can get." I slammed the phone down, feeling used and manipulated. "Is that the only reason they want me around," I thought, "so they can have a bigger group?" I have vowed that I will never intentionally become the source of that kind of pain in anyone's life.

3. Remain above reproach in everything you do.
Partiality or favoritism can kill a youth worker. We must treat everybody equally, especially when relating to the opposite sex. "Proceed with caution" becomes our banner cry. A phone call or a letter consisting of intimate language or in any way giving the appearance of a "come-on" may deal a knockout punch to our ministries. Four lifesaving words, if heeded, will preserve our reputations: *When in doubt, don't.*

five minutes and the price of a postage stamp can literally make a teenager's day come alive!

3. Be the first to acknowledge a birthday.

Most young people consider their birthdays as the single most significant day of the year. Do you have any idea how many teenagers face the agonizing reality that no one remembered their one special day? I am determined that no one in my group will ever experience this trauma again. How about in yours?

If the size of your youth group makes sending cards a cumbersome task, try recruiting some help for the mechanics of it. While requiring a minimum of administrative effort, this little venture will reap incredible dividends. Every month my secretary hands me a list of the upcoming birthdays. My wife designed a little card on which I expressed the words, "Happy Birthday! I hope you have the best one ever!" I write a brief personal greeting on each card and sign my name. My secretary hand addresses each card since a mailing label violates the personal nature of this project. Three to five minutes per card provides every person in my youth group with at least one acknowledgment of the most important day of the year.

4. Open your home for special events.

New Year's Day wouldn't be the same without our Rose Bowl Extravaganza. Everyone in the group receives a personal invitation. The only requirement—bring food or a TV. We stuff kids everywhere. Televisions blare in the bathroom, in the kitchen, on the back porch, in each bedroom, two in the garage, and one in the doghouse. To describe the scene simply as "wild" would be a classic understatement.

One year USC was trailing Ohio State by four points with five seconds on the clock. USC's quarterback threw a "Hail Mary" pass into the end zone. Just as the receiver reached up to make the game-winning catch, a girl in the group purposely pulled the plug! I've never come closer to having a teenager assassinated at any activity.

Our semimonthly desserts are nearly as famous. Five to ten young people create the perfect atmosphere in which a deepening of friendships can take place. We talk, tell stories, laugh at each other's jokes, play table games, or set up a volleyball net in the backyard.

Our greatest memories result from these evenings. Can I share just one? One of the guys thought the Jiffy Pop would cook faster if he placed the pan upside down over the flame. (After all, he reasoned, the foil on the top is far thinner than the pan on the bottom.) The flame hit the butter, then the creative chef, and he ran screaming out of the kitchen, Jiffy Pop in hand, nearly torching the house. (Oh yes, there will be times when you too will ask, "Is it really worth it all?")

5. Phone just to find out how someone is doing.

Does your mind work like mine? Whenever I receive a phone call, I instinctively wonder, "What does he want?" Only three times in thirty-five years has anyone ever called me just to say, "I was wondering how you are doing, so I thought I'd give you a call." Why not determine that you will provide that kind of phone call in someone else's life? Once again, set a realistic goal and divide your roster accordingly.

I'll never forget one of my most rewarding and fulfilling Christmas Eves. I arrived at the office early and began calling everyone in the group. I simply said, "I just called to wish you and your family the best Christmas ever!" The kids were stunned. Five hours and 150 phone calls later, my stock had risen dramatically in the eyes of my flock. For months, the young people continued to talk about their youth pastor who took time out of his Christmas Eve to make theirs a little more special.

6. Send a note of congratulations.

A daily, ten-minute scan of the local newspaper can place stories at your fingertips concerning many of the students in your youth group. These often include athletic, drama, music, or academic accomplishments. Can you imagine the impact of a congratulatory note sent in response to such an article?

7. Whenever you leave town, phone the group.

Vacations, business responsibilities, or ministry opportunities may require us to travel. These trips can provide us with the greatest opportunities to reinforce our love and commitment to our students. When you must miss a Bible study or some other activity, consider the possibility of calling your group.

Vivian, one of my students at the Master's College, was to celebrate her twenty-fifth birthday. My dear wife organized a surprise party for her at a local ice cream parlor. I was more than 100 miles away, speaking at a winter camp. I knew I would be in the middle of our evening chapel service at the time of the celebration, so I spent part of the day with the camp director installing a phone-access line. The young people arrived at 8:00. At 8:15 I called. Three hundred young people attending the chapel meeting sang their hearts out, giving a heartwarming command performance of that grand old classic, "Happy Birthday to You," over the telephone! Vivian will never enjoy a larger party! Two days later, when I returned, she grabbed me with tears in her eyes and said, "Dewey, that phone call made my birthday. I'll never forget what you did as long as I live." When the other students at the college heard what happened, my credibility skyrocketed in their eyes. Now, whenever I tell them I love them, they know my talk isn't cheap. When I teach in my classroom or in chapel, do you think the students will listen a bit more attentively? Not bad for the price of one phone call, don't you agree?

8. Answer all mail and return all phone calls.

Whenever we fail to promptly answer our mail or phone messages, we communicate one message loud and clear: "I am not interested in you."

You can answer mail with two or three sentences on a simple card. Remember, "A short letter sent is better than a long letter intended."

Phone calls can become a royal irritation. Just this morning I received ten phone messages. Returning each call potentially demands a major commitment of my time. But refusing to return a call communicates an insincere, unconcerned, and unloving attitude. Does this sound like a no-win situation?

Two principles have brought order to this otherwise time-consuming practice. First, stay in control of the call. When you must go, you must go. Determine in advance how much time you will allow for each call and stick to it. Second, return a call only once. If the person cannot be reached, simply leave a message. Your responsibility will have been fulfilled.

9. Give financial support to the young people involved in outreach and mission ministries.

The provision of money, clothing, or supplies will communicate our belief in and support of our young people far more than our words. Laura, preparing to spend her summer overseas with Teen Missions, went to her mailbox one day and nearly died of cardiac arrest. A prominent Christian leader of national recognition had sent her a support check for fifty dollars. She jumped into her van and flew over to my house, screaming all the way, "You're never going to believe this!" She was blown away. I don't think she ever even cashed it! One Christian leader's belief in Laura, expressed in the tangible form of a check, motivated her to commit her life to foreign missions. The amount of the check matters little. The fact that the support comes from us means everything.

10. Properly arrange your office.

Most offices are very sterile environments. Places of work and study do not communicate a sense of warmth and openness. I wanted to make certain that my office had a "Welcome" sign plastered right over the front. Young people need a place they can relate to as a point of identity and belonging. My office has become that place.

If you have an office at the church, have you considered hanging a bulletin board across one wall? Anything a young person gives you can become permanently enshrined for all to see. Pictures, newspaper articles, banners, and posters can be proudly displayed.

The arrangement of a desk can communicate invitation or isola-

CREATIVE METHODS OF VISITATION

An unannounced visit to a person's home typically characterizes the church visitation program. In my experience, this method only results in frustration. Rarely do I find a young person at home, and when I do, I can sense my intrusion into a messy house or hectic schedule. Creativity has turned an otherwise fruitless effort into an extremely fruitful one. Three examples stand out in my mind; you come up with your own:

- Drop in on a school-related or extracurricular activity. Athletic events, drama productions, speech contests, parades, competitions, and performances of one kind or another all qualify. A brief visit, coupled with a wave of the hand or a word of encouragement, adequately communicates to a young person our love and support.
- Stop by a student's place of employment. Make this as natural as possible and do not wear out your welcome. A quick but sincere "Hi, how was school today?" while buying a Big Mac will prove sufficient.
- Bicycle visitation has become by far the most effective method for me. My wife and I love to ride. As we pass the homes of young people we know, we'll stop and invite them to grab a bike and come along. Each time we add a young person, we ask them to point out the homes of their friends and we stop there too. We have seen groups of more than fifty young people (most of whom I had never met before) riding in caravan after only a two-hour period. We deserved a police escort!

tion. A desk placed strategically against a wall enables you to face a student with no obstacle between you. The addition of an inexpensive refrigerator can allow you to have a Coke with a student.

If you can believe it, my office recently became a Master's College dating spot! Just yesterday, three guys asked my permission to place a round patio table with chairs on a small veranda adjoining my office. They decorated the patio and set the scene for a catered, candlelit dinner for six.

I must add one very important thought. Access to an office must be regarded as a privilege, never a right. The students must clearly understand this principle: "You abuse it, you lose it." Familiarity can indeed breed contempt. A fine line exists between openness and familiarity—a line you must carefully monitor.

11. Be alert to spontaneous opportunities.
They happen every day if we train ourselves to look for them. Yesterday I walked into the snack shop at the college and bought everyone in the house a Coke. The price tag for personally touching eight students? Four dollars. Any time you and your young people happen to be in the same place—the mall, on campus, at the grocery store—you have an opportunity to give a personal touch. Good events—making a team or winning an audition—and traumatic times—illness or injury—are natural openings for personal recognition and showing you care.

12. View the personal touch as a team effort.
The goal of this chapter must be shared by the staff as a whole. No one can possibly "reach out and touch" everyone in the group on a regular basis. Frustration will surely result. No group should ever become centered on one individual. Such an arrangement would prove most unhealthy.

One of the most significant decisions I ever made in youth ministry involved dividing the larger group into smaller accountability groups, utilizing my lay staff as group leaders. I assigned each staff member from five to fifteen young people. Each leader carried the responsibility of contacting each person in their groups each week. This decision proved to be a stroke of genius! (I don't always hit the bull's-eye, but I sure did on this one!) The staff sensed a new ownership in the group. Each felt significant because I reinforced the importance of the group leader again and again. The young people no longer felt like numbers on a page or names on a roll sheet. I gained a new lease on life because I no longer carried the burden for so many young people.

By now, I am sure you understand the monumental importance of continuously striving to maintain the personal touch. While this goal may initially seem incredibly time-consuming, I assure you that your personal touch will gradually become a way of life. Every experience and situation will provide new opportunities to "reach out and touch someone." Every effort will be abundantly rewarded with a tremendous sense of fulfillment as the young people warmly and appreciatively respond.

CHECKING YOUR HEART:
A Personal EKG

1. Based on what you have just read, take evaluation of your own ministry in terms of "the personal touch." How are you doing? Which of these ideas do you now faithfully implement? List five more that you will definitely try this week.

2. The lack of a personal touch often results from the pressure to produce numbers. When the goal of youth ministry degenerates into a quest for a larger and larger group, the individual often becomes lost in the shuffle. The pressure to produce crowds will inevitably rob a group of the warmth of a personal ministry.

Do you feel this pressure? If so, turn to Matthew 16:18. Jesus said, "*I* will build My church." Allow Christ to fulfill His responsibilities while you faithfully concentrate on yours. Colossians 1:28 summarizes our primary responsibility very clearly: "And we proclaim Him, admonishing every man and teaching every man with all wisdom, that we may present every man complete in Christ." Why can't this goal be accomplished apart from the personal touch?

3. As a staff, meet together in order to set some realistic goals for "touch time." At the beginning of this chapter you read, "Every young person in every youth ministry should be given this 'touch' at least once every week." Do you agree? Why or why not?

How should they be "touched"? Can you as a staff set up some guidelines? How often should a letter be sent? How frequently should a student be contacted by phone? How do you balance the desire for showing genuine concern with creating the perception of being too pushy? What goal will each staff member set in terms of some of the more time-consuming methods (such as going out for a Coke, having students over for a dessert, etc.)? Should these questions even be considered, or should each staff member be allowed to do his own thing?

I would suggest this consideration: each staff should collectively develop a minimum commitment for each of its members. We dare not create a situation in which some young people feel cheated. Obviously, if some staff members totally neglected their accountability groups, the students as well as their leaders would suffer greatly.

4. You are not superhuman. No one can possibly carry out every idea or method listed. Get together all the leaders who work with your group, develop your own list of valid ideas, and allow each member to choose two or three to faithfully fulfill. Allow this to become a team effort. Maintaining a personal touch must be basic to the job description of every volunteer and professional youth worker.

5. List the names of ten students with whom you have lost contact over the last few months. This week, give each a call, visit their places of employment, or attend an event in which they are participating.

6. The personal touch cannot happen apart from accurate, up-to-date records. Has the time come for an update? For the next three successive Sunday mornings and midweek meetings, have the students fill out a basic information card. (Three weeks should allow for the typical turnover due to an absence.) You will need to know their names, addresses, ages, grades, schools, names of parents, and birthdays. This card should routinely be given out to everyone who visits the group.

7. How about taking a Polaroid picture of everyone in the group? Identify each person and study their faces with their names until they become indelibly imprinted upon your mind. Encourage the rest of the youth ministry team to do the same. Determine that you will greet each student by name every time you see him or her.

8. Young people follow their leaders' examples; a youth group soon takes on the personality of the staff. If you battle the common problem of cliques or an unfriendly atmosphere within the group, allow this to motivate you to pursue the personal touch with an even greater commitment. Once each leader regularly relates to the young people in a consistently personal way, the group will respond in a like manner.

8

"And Your Mother Eunice"
Maintaining a Heart for Parents

"For I am mindful of the sincere faith within you, which first dwelt in your grandmother Lois, and your mother Eunice, and I am sure that it is in you as well" (2 Timothy 1:5).

"And he will restore the hearts of the fathers to their children, and the hearts of the children to their fathers" (Malachi 4:6).

September 22, 1972, will remain etched in my mind until the day I die. I've never been more nervous in all my life. A gathering of some fifty parents crowded into the rather small room, their first bona fide look at the new youth pastor. All of twenty years old, I was woefully inexperienced in youth ministry, or any other ministry for that matter.

As I entered the room, things seemed cordial enough. Most parents smiled, though some gave a few disconcerting stares. At precisely 7 P.M. I called the meeting to order. My hands shook and my voice quivered as I attempted to explain the reasons for my calling the parents together.

I was just beginning to feel comfortable when suddenly, at the back of the room, the door flew open and in walked Mrs. Jacobs. I couldn't miss her. No one could. She wasn't particularly obese, but certainly big enough to create a stir. She ambled over to a chair in the front row, in front of my podium, and captured the attention of everyone in the room. She leaned back, gave a sigh that unmistakably communicated boredom, and mockingly called out at the top of her voice, "OK, Dewey, tell me how to raise my kids." My very first parent meeting had begun.

No, I'm definitely not masochistic. So why subject myself to such abuse? Because the most effective youth ministry you and I will ever do will flow out of a ministry to parents. Parent ministry constitutes a major youth ministry nonnegotiable. Nothing has proven as important in my fifteen years of experience as an ongoing ministry to parents.

WHY MINISTER TO PARENTS?

First, God has given the primary authority over children to their parents (Deuteronomy 6:6-7; Ephesians 6:1-4). He did not place the church or the youth worker in this position.

I can anticipate an immediate response to that statement. Some would ask, "But what if the parents fail to fulfill their God-ordained role? Shouldn't we then step in as youth workers and become a sort of surrogate parent?" Absolutely not! God can accomplish His purposes even through an imperfect parent. Understanding the proper place of parental authority will free us to fulfill our role properly as youth workers.

Last Sunday morning, a mother came to church to hear me

preach. As she greeted me at the door, she suddenly burst into tears and hugged me for a rather prolonged period of time. As people stopped and stared, I tried to smile through my embarrassment, but could only think, "Why me?" I felt like I had to say something, so I asked, "How's Gloria [her daughter]? I haven't seen her in a while." Through her tears she said, "That's why I came to see you this morning. When I heard you were speaking here today, I just had to come and tell you how well she's doing." Then she stopped crying and looked me right in the eyes as she said, "Dewey, thank you for always being there for her, and thank you most of all for being there for my husband and me." Two thoughts flashed through my mind: (1) This family has sure experienced their share of struggles. (2) The results could have been disastrous had I violated the proper role of a youth worker in relation to parental authority. What is a youth worker's proper role? Keep reading.

Second, the local church exists as a support to the family, never as a replacement. Youth workers enjoy a privileged position—we can offer our assistance in enabling the parents to become the best possible. Kellie Coleman, one of my students, coined the perfect label when she said, "Youth workers are to function as 'paraparents.' " From the Greek preposition *para,* paraparents defines our role as that of literally "coming alongside" the parents, offering the best source of support they will find anywhere. "Even at twenty years of age and lacking in experience?" you might ask. Absolutely. I'll tell you how in a moment.

Finally, with all of the destructive forces aimed at the youth of our day, a united front has become an essential ingredient. Our ultimate effectiveness, as youth workers or parents may depend upon our concerted effort to gain an influence in the homes of our youth. We have no choice but to try.

ESTABLISHING A MINISTRY TO PARENTS

Where do we begin? What if we have no experience in the rearing of children, let alone teenagers? What if our limited time has already been stretched to the limits? What if we cannot get the parents to respond?

Surprisingly enough, as difficult as these questions may seem, the establishment and maintenance of a ministry to parents need not be difficult. Several important guidelines show us the overall picture and help us get a handle on what to do and why.

1. Carefully assess your priorities and time commitment.

"Will the real Superman please stand up?" Don't hold your breath. No one is standing. Neither you nor I will ever fill his shoes. You cannot possibly do everything people suggest, and neither can I. There comes a breaking point in ministry, a moment of truth, at which we must acknowledge the fact that some things, some very good things, may have to remain undone.

We can get along with fewer social activities. A visitation program would be nice, but perhaps the penetration of school campuses will fulfill this dimension of ministry. Not every church needs a youth choir or basketball team. We would all love to offer these programs and many others. At some point, however, we will either choose to operate within a very carefully defined system of priorities or we will burn out. A ministry to parents must be classified as one of these priorities.

Like so many things in ministry, a parent ministry can be very simple or extremely complex. Let me suggest that you begin with the basics and allow the ministry to evolve gradually. I can assure you that the ideas presented in this chapter will not require excessive amounts of time, preparation, or administrative skill.

2. Set the proper goal.

What do we wish to accomplish? Here is the goal I have set: "A ministry to parents exists in order to provide the best forum in which I can communicate my sincere loyalty and love to each parent represented in my youth ministry." As we work toward this goal, we will encounter at least three common pitfalls.

We may experience frustration over the lack of parental response. Generally speaking, in spite of my best efforts, only one third to one half of the parents will come to any given event to which they are invited. Many parents simply don't care. Others have misplaced priorities. Some believe that they do not need our input or support. While we may feel an intense disappointment over those who do not respond, our efforts must focus on our opportunities to influence those who do respond.

We may be tempted to give up. Hard or indifferent hearts will not soften overnight. One individual told me in no uncertain terms that he was not interested. Even though his two daughters received Christ and experienced dramatic changes in their lives, he would not budge. Four years later, at the age of fifty-two, he discovered that he had terminal cancer and less than one year to live. He fought and resisted, refusing to believe his doctor's diagnosis. Finally, while in his hospital bed, two days before he died, he prayed to receive Christ. How tragic it would have been if we had given up on him too soon.

We may place ourselves under unnecessary pressure. Remember, we are not presenting ourselves to the parents as God's all-time answer to the family dilemma. I expend enough energy in the rearing of my two children without taking on the responsibility of telling other people how to raise theirs. Our goal is on the building of relationships through which our care and support can be expressed. Parents can get the answers they need from a book. But a book will hardly qualify as a substitute for a caring heart—something you and I can certainly provide.

3. Begin to formulate some functional ideas.

Let's get practical. What does a ministry to parents look like? Exactly what should we do? I can suggest several ideas based upon my ministry to parents. Evaluate them in light of your own unique situation. Allow these thoughts to spark your thinking as you determine the best way to meet the needs of the parents with whom you work.

• Send a personal letter. Every parent represented in my ministry receives a personal letter from me every year. I express my sincere appreciation to the parents for the privilege they have granted me by allowing their son or daughter to be a part of my ministry. I assure them that I do not take this privilege lightly.

Next, I remind them that our church desires to support their family in any way possible as they seek to instill character and convictions in the lives of their children. I never use the word *help.* I do not want to imply or assume that they have a problem. The word *support* creates a positive perception, conveying my ongoing commitment to care for the well-being of their family.

I also renew my pledge to recognize and honor their authority in

GOALS FOR A PARENT MEETING

- To meet personally with each parent for the purpose of building a relationship;
- To provide information concerning the philosophy and direction of the youth ministry;
- To communicate the details of upcoming Bible studies and activities;
- To reinforce support for their role in the rearing of their children;
- To create a sense of accountability as they share feedback concerning the strengths and weaknesses of the youth ministry;
- To generate an atmosphere in which the parents can begin to support one another;
- To pray together as a group of people striving for the same goals;
- To form a resource pool for equipment, homes for Bible studies or activities, and helpers for certain upcoming events;
- To expose the parents to various aspects and trends in contemporary youth culture that may impact their teenagers;
- To silence the critics. Invariably, those who criticize us will come from the ranks of people who do not bother to attend the parent meetings. Naturally, they will not understand our philosophy or direction. If they should attack, we can simply but respectfully point out that they have not been in attendance and, therefore, cannot properly evaluate the ministry.

the lives of their children. I want them to know that I will never purposely contradict anything they may decide for their children. I am assuming the best here. I believe that most parents, including unbelievers, want their children to grow up with a semblance of character and to live productive lives. I will certainly not support a parent's decision to have his son or daughter violate a clear command of Scripture. Since this situation rarely occurs, I need not address it in this letter.

If you choose to implement this idea, please make certain that you personally address each letter. Never use a mailing label and do not send the letter "To the parents of. . . . " Continually update your information. Often the parents do not carry the same last name as their children, or you may be dealing with a broken home, a foster home, or guardianship.

• Offer regular parent meetings. If I had time to incorporate only one idea from this chapter, I would select this one. Hold them monthly or quarterly, depending on your own time constraints. Follow a flexible format, tailor-made to suit your particular situation. One year we met at the church on the first Monday of every month in a large group of 150 parents. One year we divided the parents into three groups and met with one group each month in the intimacy of a home. I prefer a smaller group meeting in the warmth of a living room.

To illustrate the possible structure of a parent meeting, let me suggest a typical schedule: From 7:00–7:15 P.M., give information concerning upcoming events and your teaching plan for the month. From 7:15–7:45, teach some aspect of youth culture. Keep in mind that parents usually do not understand the teenage world or the characteristics of teenagers in general. They have been exposed only to their own son or daughter. From 7:45–8:00, pray together. And from 8:00–8:30, throw it open for questions and answers. Serve refreshments at 8:30 and enjoy an informal time of talking.

• Make available all lesson plans and youth meeting outlines. Tape-record all messages and sermons. Parents have the right to monitor their teenagers' spiritual input. This kind of openness maintains a sense of accountability to the parents concerning our teaching. Whenever a question or concern arises over something we have said, a review of the tape will always settle the issue.

You may be surprised to learn that some students will enthusiastically share the tapes with their friends, extending your influence even further. I even discovered a cure for insomnia! One dear, well-meaning mother was beside herself with excitement when she called me on the phone. "I haven't been able to sleep for weeks," she explained. "Last night my daughter gave me one of your tapes saying, 'Mom, you've just got to hear him.' Well, I turned it on and lay down to listen. By your second point, I was sound asleep!" So, you never know!

BENEFITS OF PARENT MINISTRY

For a small investment of time, you will find that:

- the parents will give you your greatest source of encouragement and support;
- you will experience a minimum of criticism;
- you will enjoy a healthy rapport with the parents;
- the young people receive a greater freedom to participate in the ministry.

• Teach on the topic of authority. Questions concerning parental authority abound in the minds of today's teenagers. "Why did God place me under parental authority? When does that authority end? Does submission imply blind obedience? Am I ever right in disobeying my parents? How do I handle it when I just don't agree with them?" We must tackle these and similar questions in our teaching ministry. We must also be careful to model what we teach by our own proper responses to those in authority over us. As the young people learn from our exposition and example, the resulting changes at home will do more to validate our influence than anything else we do.

Would you like to hear a classic example of this principle in action? Jackie's father exploded when he found out I wanted to meet him. "I don't want that man to ever come around this house again!" She called me on the phone, feeling frantic over her father's anger. He couldn't accept his daughter's newfound faith in Christ and chose to take his frustration out on me. I calmly told her to consistently display an attitude of respect toward her father. I demonstrated the same respect by backing way off. Jackie's attitude in the home did more to soften her father's heart than anything I could have said or done. In time, he and I built a fairly close friendship. When a young man from our church sought permission to marry Jackie, her father asked me what I thought. I'll never forget what he said: "I cannot allow my daughter to marry someone you do not approve of."

• Accurately communicate the details of all activities and stick to them. Trust must be earned, and this takes time. A friend of mine had to learn the hard way. Summer camp had ended and the young people anticipated a seven-hour drive. Halfway home, an engine hose burst, and fifty students found themselves stranded. Sound familiar? The driver left the bus, hitchhiked to the nearest gas station, and bought the part he needed. By the time they got the bus back on the road, they had been delayed four hours. The parents expected the bus to arrive at 7 P.M. Several sat in the church parking lot and waited. By 9:00, many were extremely worried. By 10:00, a few became hysterical. A couple of families vowed never to let their young people attend any more outings with the church again.

My friend's response sounded painfully pathetic. Place yourself in the position of a parent and tell me if his words sound hollow. "Well, I couldn't help it if the bus blew a hose." True enough. But why didn't he just telephone a responsible adult and have him meet the parents in order to explain the cause of the delay and give the location of the bus and an approximate time of arrival? Such an action would have built trust. His neglect and insensitivity to the feelings of the parents struck an enormous blow to his credibility.

- Invite parents to a regular youth meeting. Try to keep the flow of the evening as close to a typical meeting as possible. You might want to include in the program two or three young people who have compelling testimonies. Has your ministry been a particular encouragement to any families in your church? Have a parent tell about it.

Showcase your staff. Introduce each one and briefly explain his or her particular role within the overall ministry. Have the parents wear name tags in order to encourage interaction. Select three or four couples to welcome new parents. And, of course, provide refreshments. Have you noticed the direct correlation between the quality of the food and the numbers in attendance?

What do you hope to accomplish? The parents will get an accurate picture of a typical youth meeting. A nonthreatening environment will have been provided for the unchurched parents. They will hear firsthand of the youth ministry's impact both in the lives of individual young people and in families as a whole. An opportunity can be given for people to receive Christ. Parents who may be on the fringe will be exposed to the ministries of the church. And parents who formerly did not know one another will meet each other. Not too bad for one night's work!

- Plan occasional parent/teen outings. Anytime we can create an opportunity to deepen the relationship between a parent and a teenager, we witness a momentous achievement. These activities can take the place of a regular social so as to not add significantly to your already overworked schedule.

The ideas abound. We recently hosted a "Downhill Derby." We found the longest and steepest hill available and sponsored a soapbox derby. You wouldn't believe some of the vehicles these families came up with! We posted only three guidelines: the vehicles must have at least three wheels, a braking system, but no power source. The event ended with a family picnic and softball game.

You will want to exercise sensitivity to those young people who do not live with both parents. No one should ever feel left out or second-class because of his family situation. Obviously, stepparents or guardians should be included. When a teenager has no one to bring, perhaps an older man or woman in church could adopt the young person for the day. He or she may want to become a genuine friend and prayer partner with the student throughout the year.

4. Start small and allow the ministry to expand naturally.

I have given a wealth of information in this chapter; don't feel overwhelmed or intimidated. You don't need to incorporate these ideas all at once. Assess your time commitments and the needs of your group and design the parent ministry accordingly. Do what you can when you can. Feel your way along. If something works, do it again. If something bombs, at least you tried. But don't give up. Over time, you will begin to sense what works with your group and what doesn't. You will see progress. And no matter how you define it, progress constitutes success.

Let me summarize this chapter. Many youth pastors have said to me, "I'm so busy I cannot afford to begin a parent ministry." You can anticipate my response: I'm so busy I cannot afford not to. I desperately need their support, trust, and encouragement; and they need mine. Think it through and begin the adventure. As a youth pastor friend of mine shared with me not long ago, "Setting up a monthly meeting with the parents is by far the smartest thing I've ever done!"

CHECKING YOUR HEART:
A Personal EKG

1. Realistically assess your current time commitments. Do you have time to undertake this dimension of ministry? If not, keep a written record of everything you do this next week. List each activity and assign a number to each based on its importance in light of your overall ministry. Where on your list does a ministry to parents fit in terms of its relative importance? Which of the lesser priority items can you eliminate in order to make time for this one?

2. Have you become convinced of the importance of a parent ministry? Are you ministering to parents now? If so, what positive benefits have resulted? What changes do you need to make in order to increase your effectiveness?

If you do not currently have a ministry to parents, ask yourself, "Why not?" Can you give a valid reason? Objectively list the pros and cons of starting such a ministry. After weighing the two sides, can you put off a ministry to parents any longer?

3. Don't try to do it alone. You can easily distribute the administration of parent meetings or the writing of personal letters among the youth ministry team. If you are the only youth worker in your church, can you think of someone in the congregation who might have a heart for these kinds of projects?

4. Parents can form another pool of potential ministry support. Think about the parents represented in your ministry. Can you think of any with particular strengths beneficial to your ministry? Can you identify tasks a parent could accomplish? Be prepared to utilize them. The more individuals who "own" the youth ministry, the more effective it will become.

5. From the ideas listed in this chapter, select two or three you might implement this year. Take out a sheet of paper and write down every conceivable task that must be accomplished in order for the idea to become reality. For example, if you chose to have a parent meeting, you will need a place to meet, a date, refreshments, publicity, perhaps certain equipment, handouts, etc. Ask for volunteers to fulfill each task. In the beginning, keep the project simple. In time, as the benefits of the ministry grow, people will offer their assistance with enthusiasm.

6. I cannot overemphasize the importance of updated records. Evaluate the present condition of your records. Do you sense the need for some overhauling? If so, what steps will you take to make your records accurate? The most important entries include the first and last names of each parent along with their addresses and phone numbers.

7. If you try and fail, don't become discouraged. Remember, if something doesn't work, evaluate what went wrong and try again. Failure occurs only when we give up. Remember Thomas Edison, who made 5,000 unsuccessful attempts to invent the light bulb? He was asked, "Aren't you getting discouraged?" He replied, "Are you kidding? Not for one second. I've just discovered 5,000 ways it won't work." We shall indeed "in due time reap if we do not grow weary" (Galatians 6:9).

9

"Of Kindred Spirit"
Maintaining a Heart for Volunteer Staff

"But I hope in the Lord Jesus to send Timothy to you shortly . . . for I have no one else of kindred spirit" (Philippians 2:19-20).

"And He gave some as apostles, and some as prophets, and some as evangelists, and some as pastors and teachers, for the equipping of the saints for the work of service, to the building up of the body of Christ" (Ephesians 4:11-12).

Let's play a word association game. I'll give you a word and you respond with the first word that pops into your mind. Ready? *Baseball.* What did you think of? *Hot dogs? Home runs? The World Series? Babe Ruth? The Hall of Fame?*

Whenever I hear the word *baseball,* for some strange reason I immediately think of Tommy Lasorda. True, for years he has managed the Los Angeles Dodgers, and I happen to live in the Los Angeles area. But I think of Lasorda primarily because of a profound comment he once made in response to a reporter's praise of his managing ability: "The fact of the matter is this—the team could show up on the field without me, play the game, and win. But if I showed up without them, I'd lose. I need the players much more than they need me." I thought to myself, "Right on, Tommy. You've just summarized perfectly my sentiments regarding my volunteer staff."

Let's go back to our word association game. Try the phrase *youth ministry.* Whenever I hear those words, my mind spins like a floppy disk and spews out words like *exciting, challenging, fulfilling, exhilarating, heartbreaking, exhausting, relentlessly demanding, draining, humanly impossible, help!, pressure, I can't do this alone!* Truer words have never been spoken—I need my volunteer staff far more than they need me.

Can we play our little word association game once more? This time, let's tackle the phrase *In the beginning. . . .* Let me guess. The words *God created the heavens and the earth* just flashed across your frontal lobes. Not so with me. I just relived a nightmare.

In the beginning of my youth ministry, I had no kids, no experience, and no staff. I started completely from scratch. Sound typical? Out of desperation I cried out to the Lord of the harvest to send laborers into His harvest. For nine frightfully long months I labored alone as best I could. Eventually, God gave me one of the most priceless gifts possible when He sent Ron and Stephanie Jones. I owe my survival in the ministry to this faithful couple. In time, others joined our ranks: Gary Walters, Carole Lawton, Ed and Laura Tooley, Dan and Teri Sumner, Dan and Valerie Mejia, Pam Richmond, and several others. Looking back over fifteen years of ministry, I can tell you that I needed each one of them far more than they needed me.

Where do good quality staff come from? What should you look for

BENEFITS OF A VOLUNTEER STAFF

Having a volunteer staff allows the youth pastor to:

- train lay people in youth ministry by providing hands-on experience;
- insulate himself against the loneliness of ministry;
- create a sense of personal accountability as his staff watches every move he makes;
- share his responsibilities;
- extend his influence as he reproduces himself in the lives of his staff;
- benefit from the gifts and talents of several people who have committed themselves to the same goals;
- provide the young people with a variety of individuals to whom they can go for counsel and encouragement;
- maintain the personal nature of the group in the midst of growth;
- expose the young people to differing personalities; acknowledging the fact that not every teenager will "click" with just anyone;
- create a forum from which creative ideas, plans, and decisions can flow.

in selecting a staff? What should you do once you've found them? How do you keep them once they are part of the team?

KEYS TO TEAMWORK

While many of my comments will be directed to the youth pastor, all the members of the volunteer staff must be like-minded in the understanding of the role of the layperson in youth ministry. Whether you are a paid youth worker or a lay staff member, you will benefit greatly from this chapter. We shall consider all of the factors essential to the effective mobilization of the lay staff.

1. Maintain the proper perspective.

The staff does not exist for the youth pastor. The youth pastor exists for the staff. Many youth pastors make a fatal mistake at precisely this point. Anyone who serves in a staff position must be viewed as a person to be mobilized, not merely a tool to be used. Please make note of two critically important misconceptions.

The first misconception is that the youth pastor needs a lay staff in order to best fulfill his or her goals. No way! A youth pastor must never sketch out a program and then recruit staff people to make it fly. Such a perception immediately removes a staff member's sense of personal worth and dignity, reducing him to a mere pawn.

One of my close friends who became a youth pastor inherited an incredible staff. During one of his first meetings, he laid out his plans and said, "This is the program, ladies and gentlemen. If you don't like it, you can leave it. There's no room for disloyal people here." The end result? Within three months, half of his staff became disillusioned and left; within five months, he himself was fired.

My staff does not exist to fulfill my goals. I exist to discover their goals and do all I can to equip and support them, helping their objectives become reality. They do not exist to make me successful; I exist to make them successful. Effective leadership never results from lording it over people but rather from serving people.

The second misconception is that the youth pastor needs a lay staff in order to lighten his or her load. Not so. Some people salivate at the thought of a group of people to whom they can delegate, thinking all the while that they will finally be able to sit back and watch the ministry happen. If that summarizes your thinking, note this carefully. We will never have a light load no matter how big a staff we may have. We must build a multiple staff with multiple gifts and goals because an effective ministry to teenagers must be multifaceted. Our efforts have nothing to do with getting out from a load of work.

Do the gifts of a multiple staff necessarily result in a comprehensive youth ministry? No, and that does not bother me. No individual group or church can possibly touch every conceivable need represented in a city. I have no goals concerning the formation of new ministries. I have left that with the Holy Spirit. I am concerned about equipping each staff member to pursue his or her wildest dreams while enjoying a measure of effectiveness. When a youth pastor sets that as the goal, the staff will become the most excited and fulfilled bunch around. Talk about a sense of personal worth coupled with an ownership of the youth ministry? They will have it!

GIFT-BASED MINISTRY

A college-age girl came to me and said, "I want so badly to work with young people, but I don't know what I have to offer." I asked her to tell me something about her background and discovered that as a teenager she had become involved in an immoral relationship. She began to cry as she told me of the agony and guilt of having an abortion. Then she said, "If only someone could get to these pregnant girls early enough to give them the support they need." Bingo! Why couldn't that "someone" be this girl? At my suggestion, her eyes lit up and she said, "You mean that God can use my awful past to help someone now?" That day we began a ministry to pregnant teenagers in our city.

One of my staff guys had dropped out of high school. He understands the mind-set of a dropout. He can relate to feelings of inferiority, failure, and worthlessness; he's been there. When he joined my staff, he said, "I don't suppose you have any use for a dropout, do you?" Are you kidding? He now heads up a ministry to dropouts while penetrating the continuation schools in our city.

Mark played football in high school. He understands the mind-set of an athlete. He began an outreach to the football team. Ed had a burden for following up new believers. He began a new believer's Bible study. The same thing happened with a ministry to young people living in broken homes, a ministry to parents, small-group discipleship, a visitation ministry, and a drama team. Each ministry began as a burden in the heart of one of my staff members. As you can see, the program does not determine each staff member's responsibilities; each staff member determines the program.

2. Establish your standards.

Please, never violate this principle. We will always face the temptation of allowing less-than-qualified individuals join the staff because, quite frankly, most of us desperately need help. I had to learn the hard way; let me spare you months of agony. Underline this statement and never forget it: *Better to have a few qualified staff people than many unqualified ones.* I'll tell you why.

Nothing will drain our energy faster than the pressure of having to motivate a slothful staff person. We simply do not have time to pick up the pieces every time he falters. We need people who will faithfully fulfill their responsibilities the first time, even without direct supervision.

Second, insincere motives abound. Many people will jump on the bandwagon for the wrong reasons.

Some perceive youth ministry as a glamour position. If they only knew! As soon as the glamour fades and good, old-fashioned hard work sets in, these will be the first to bail out and hit the road.

For some, an involvement with teenagers becomes a feeble attempt at preserving their own youthfulness. (What's that old line? "If you want to stay young, run with the young." Of course, they forget "If you want to die young, try to keep up with them!")

For some, the pedestal looks appealing. They long to have little groupies gather at their feet and worship them as a hero of the faith.

A few will come around simply because they don't seem to fit in anywhere else. Having been social outcasts on their peer level, they move down a notch and try to make it with teenagers.

A final reason for maintaining high standards for staff is that in general the young people will never experience a greater level of spiritual commitment than that of the staff. Whenever we introduce a new staff person to my group, we communicate a message to our young people loud and clear: "If you want to know how to live a Christian life, live like him or her." Unqualified staff members make lousy models. Their examples will subtly but certainly erode the character and convictions we seek to build into our teenagers. And unfortunately, it's always easier to hire than fire.

What constitutes the proper standard for a youth staff member? The typical answer? We want FAT people (Faithful, Available, and Teachable). Not bad. However, this needs some definition.

In 1 Timothy 4, Paul clearly defined the characteristics of the "good servant of Christ Jesus." These characteristics have been examined in detail in the first two chapters of this book. You may wish to review those chapters at this point.

You may be thinking, "Where will I find staff people like this?"

Admittedly, we must make one concession. Many potential staff members will be young, both chronologically and spiritually. Consequently, they may not have consistently developed every one of these qualities in their lives. (Don't let that shock you; neither have I.) God is not looking for *perfection*. He is concerned about the *direction* of our lives. Aren't you glad? We must ask ourselves one very important question about prospective staff members: "Are they seeking to live up to the characteristics of 1 Timothy 4?" If so, they qualify. If not, we cannot allow them to serve on the youth staff at this time. Their desire for involvement in the youth ministry may, in time, sufficiently motivate them to bring their lives in line with the biblical standard. A volunteer staff application form (see Appendix F) may be helpful in emphasizing the importance of the position to prospective staff. We would do a great disservice both to them and to our young people if we accepted them when they are less than qualified.

3. Do not recruit staff.

Sound a bit strange? Let me explain my terms. I define *recruitment* as making mass appeals while manipulating people to involve themselves in the youth ministry of their church. Bulletin blurbs and pulpit pleadings will invariably result in a plethora of responses from well-meaning but unqualified individuals. Begging, pleading, coercing, intimidating, or manipulating should never characterize our style. I decided a long time ago that I would no longer approach the unmotivated; I would rather have the motivated approach me.

While this may look good on paper, the burning question becomes, "How do I get someone—anyone—to approach me?" Consider these five possibilities.

First, give high visibility to the youth ministry. People will often become attracted to ministries which evidence the moving of the hand of God. Bulletin announcements, youth newsletters (we called ours "Spotlight on Youth"), youth testimonies in the worship services, youth night services, baptismal services, and word-of-mouth reports can contribute to the excitement of the congregation concerning the blessing of God upon the youth ministry.

Second, utilize the principle of "planned neglect." Until God begins to raise up staff, boil the ministry down to the bare essentials and give yourself wholly to the most important tasks. (I should think that Bible studies, parent meetings, and campus involvement would certainly qualify as "the most important tasks.")

Never fall into the trap of imitating the guy in the circus who tries to spin 100 plates on 100 poles. You'll burn out in a second. And you will find, much to your own frustration, that people will let you do everything if you seem willing. By purposely neglecting potential ministry possibilities, we will allow people to visualize ways in which they can make a much-needed contribution to the overall youth program.

When someone tells me, "You need to have small-group discipleship for the really committed kids," I routinely respond by saying, "Thank God that He has finally laid that burden on someone's heart. I have been praying that God would raise someone up to oversee that much-needed aspect of this ministry. You may be God's answer to my prayer." One of two things happens—he climbs on board, or I've silenced a potential critic. Ephesians 4:11-12 springs to life as we commit ourselves, not to doing every conceivable task, but to the equipping of the saints (lay staff) to do the work of the ministry!

Third, utilize the parents for short-term support. Parent meetings will quickly prove their worth! While most parents may not want to take on the responsibilities of a full-fledged staff member, they may feel honored to have a part in a one-time event.

Fourth, keep your eyes open for "the naturals." You may meet individuals along the way whose pores ooze with youth ministry ability. They may never come forward. They may wait for you to come to them.

What should we do in this case? I love to conduct business over a meal (something about "a way to a person's heart . . ."). During the course of conversation, tell the person what you have observed. "Jim, I am acquainted with several youth staff members. I know what it takes to minister effectively to young people. And Jim, there's no doubt about it. You've got what it takes." Having stated your premise, specifically point out the qualities you have observed.

Your comments will have the ring of credibility to them if you meet two criteria: (1) Your heart obviously burns with a passion for young people. Since youth ministry ranks in your life as a sky-high priority, people will understand that you will not be throwing around a lot of fluff. They will quickly come to realize that these conversations are important. (2) You do *not* have the reputation of using high-pressure techniques to recruit staff. Your reputation as one who seeks quality over quantity will cause anyone to feel honored rather than suspicious about your approach.

Fifth, pray continually for the Lord of the harvest to raise up workers. Ultimately, God must lay the burden on a person's heart. Our faithful prayer coupled with an obvious enthusiasm and passion for young people will provide a powerful one-two punch in terms of influencing quality men and women to join the team. Be patient. Time will always be required to find the best.

4. Have your needs clearly in mind.

Most people who approach us about staff involvement will not have pinpointed the exact niche they want to fill. We can assist them by providing a list of needs we believe they can fulfill.

Meet with a prospective staff member over the privacy of a meal (your treat). Mention three or four needs you have identified in the ministry at the present time. Allow him time to pray over each opportunity before responding. He may become excited about one of the possibilities, or he may offer a proposal of his own. If his idea does not violate a biblical absolute, if it seems valid in terms of the overall direction of the youth ministry, and if he has developed a plan to fulfill it, tell him, "Go for it." God will have just added a new dimension to the youth ministry!

5. Provide a clearly defined job description.

People become frustrated when they feel unclear about their specific roles. For each staff member, type out his exact responsibilities, including the frequency with which he must attend meetings, activities, and Bible studies. (A sample volunteer-staff contract can be found in Appendix G.)

I have always operated on a one-year commitment basis. This prevents the feeling of burnout that can result from a demanding, ongoing, and never-ending responsibility—a natural break will be forthcoming. If he chooses to step aside after fulfilling his initial commitment, he will not feel as if he let us down. If he chooses to stay, a new one-year contract can be negotiated (certain changes in the job description may be beneficial). A one-year commitment will also allow for a natural and peaceful method of eliminating an unqualified or uncommitted staff person.

6. Give each staff person an accountability group.

Every young person must be held accountable by a staff person. Lone rangers do not last.

Accountability should not be confused with discipleship. Discipleship can be defined as the reproduction of ourselves in another through a personal commitment of time and teaching. Accountability involves our checking up on a teenager in terms of his spiritual well-being. Calling him on occasion, taking him out for a Coke once in a while, monitoring his attendance, and offering him words of encouragement all fall under the category of accountability. We can't maintain the personal touch without this.

I have used a ratio of eight to twelve young people per staff person when the size of the staff permits this. The students should be assigned (guys with men and girls with women) on the basis of geography (living in close proximity to one's young people can have tremendous advantages) and ministry (a staff member who has a burden for teens from broken homes should have an accountability group consisting of young people coming from this background).

7. Provide regular staff training.

The significance of this principle cannot be overstated. Three dynamics take place all at once: the staff will learn our unique philosophical approach to youth ministry; we will be able to clearly communicate our continual commitment and support to each of them; and they will have the opportunity to ask questions about specific ministry problems while sharing their victories with one another.

The timing of these meetings will be critical. Try to avoid an additional night out. You don't need it and neither do they. One hour before the midweek Bible study may prove ideal.

8. Understand the principles of delegation.

Effective leadership demands the mastery of delegation. Those who have, by their own personal choice or by default, become trapped into doing everything themselves will most certainly self-destruct.

While entire books have been written on the subject, a consideration of five basic principles will prove sufficient for our purposes.

First, delegate anything that someone else can do. Our time should be devoted to the projects we do best. Identify the tasks that someone else can effectively perform and give them away.

Second, delegate only to willing individuals. Find someone with a heart for the responsibility in question. We would do far better in allowing a task to remain undone than to force it upon an unwilling staff member. Nothing will sap strength and enthusiasm faster.

Third, create the recognition of a team ministry. The staff must understand that their fulfillment of assigned responsibilities will free us up to do what we do best. The motive of our delegation must never be perceived as personal laziness.

Fourth, periodically check in with the people to whom tasks have been delegated. Constantly offer encouragement, advice, and support. Remember, even though certain tasks have been assigned, the ultimate responsibility for their fulfillment continues to lie with us.

Fifth, praise them along the way. Constantly remind the staff of their invaluable contribution to the overall goal of the youth ministry. Help them to see the big picture. They are doing far more than making cookies for the upcoming "Saturday Night Special." They are helping to change the world!

9. Do fun things together as a staff.

We labor together, fight the battles together, laugh together, cry together, get exhausted and burn out together, live together, and at times die together. But through it all, we ought to have a lot of fun together. Check out a few concrete examples from my own staff experiences.

We always hold our monthly staff meetings in a home around a potluck meal. Our greatest times of interaction come as we gather around a pizza in someone's backyard or living room. At the conclusion of our meeting, we head to a park for a game of softball, football, or ultimate frisbee. The staff meetings have been transformed from a drudgery to a delight.

Two staff retreats highlight each year. Generally three days and two nights in length, we purposely program an equal amount of work time and playtime.

Birthdays, Christmas, and certain holidays provide us with added opportunities to get together just for the fun of it.

Through these and similar ideas, we have become an extremely close-knit circle of friends who just happen to minister on the same team together. Not only does this approach balance the seriousness and intensity of ministry, but we provide the young people with a living, breathing model of true unity and love among believers in Christ.

CHECKING YOUR HEART:
A Personal EKG

1. Let's evaluate. Invite each staff member over for dinner and discuss the following questions:

a. What ministries are we currently offering to the young people now?

b. Can we brainstorm several possible ministries we would love to see God raise up in the future? (Dream big. Don't allow yourself any limits. Think through every conceivable need and situation faced by the young people in your city.) How about these for starters?

- Outreach teams
- Ministry to runaways
- Ministry to drug abusers
- Ministry to juvenile halls in your area
- Ministry to foster children
- Ministry to unwed mothers
- Ministry to girls who have had abortions
- Ministry to teenagers struggling with homosexuality
- Drama team
- Youth choir
- Ministry to the athletic teams at the schools
- Ministry to public school teachers
- Summer missions projects
- Campus penetration
- New believer's Bible studies
- Ministry to parents
- Ministry to the handicapped
- Small-group discipleship
- Camping ministry

You will find no limit to the possibilities. Do you sense a need for restructuring your present youth ministry? Are staff involved in any activities simply for the sake of doing them, rather than because of a heartfelt passion? Should some current ministries be dropped and others added? Have you fallen into the trap of formulating a preset youth program while trying to find warm bodies to staff it? These questions should make for an interesting evening's discussion!

2. In lieu of recruiting staff:

a. Determine creative methods of informing the congregation about the youth ministry.

b. Formulate a list of specific needs that can be presented as matters of prayer before the people.

c. Ask yourself, "Which vitally important aspects of the youth ministry are currently being neglected because of a staff shortage?" Can the parents assist in any way? Be prepared to make an appeal at your next parent meeting.

d. Organize a regular prayer meeting in which you and any other staff members can ask God for His blessing on the youth ministry of your church as well as for the raising up of quality staff.

e. Remember the priority of ministry: It is far better to do a few things (even one thing!) with excellence than many things with mediocrity.

3. Have the current staff members been given clearly defined job descriptions? Does each person understand his role? Does he know the expectations that have been placed upon him in terms of attendance and performance? Can he visualize how his involvement contributes to the overall ministry? Has this become an area of frustration among the staff? If so, drop everything and attack this head-on. A job description, properly worded, will promote staff unity, minimize tensions, and create a sense of security and identity for each staff member.

4. Loyalty becomes the glue that holds a staff together. Each staff person must know that everyone else on staff would die for him if need be. Do you experience any friction on staff, brought about by a lack of mutual loyalty and support? Is gossip tolerated? When someone comes to a staff member to complain about another on staff, is the person allowed to spread his criticism? Is there a freedom to confront one another in spirit of Galatians 6 whenever a biblical absolute has been violated? If staff unity has become a problem, set up a staff meeting and study the following passages together: Proverbs 6:16-19, James 3:1-12, Ephesians 4:25-32, and Galatians 6:1-15. Memorize together Proverbs 13:3, 15:1-4, 18:8, Matthew 12:36, Ephesians 4:29, and James 1:26.

5. How about staff training? What would they like by way of regular input? Set up a time and begin. This book would be an excellent place to start. Bring in experts from time to time to lecture concerning certain specialized aspects of youth culture (drug abuse, suicide prevention, abortion alternatives, etc.).

6. Think through the entire issue of delegation. As a staff, discuss the success or failure of the principles given in this chapter. How do the members of the staff feel when a task is assigned to them? Excited? Resentful? Do they sense that they are victimized by someone else's laziness, or do they genuinely feel as though they are freeing others up to do what they do best? Do they enthusiastically go for it because they want to change their world, or has someone failed in giving them the big picture?

7. If you haven't already, start having fun together. If you have followed through on the first six projects mentioned, cast the book aside at this point, grab a bat and ball, and go for broke for a couple of hours.

Every Wednesday from 1:00 to 2:30 P.M., the Bible department faculty at the Master's College play softball together—just for the fun of it. An investment of 1½ hours per week has revolutionized the department! Sometimes we can take life a little too seriously. If we don't balance the intensity of ministry with some lighthearted fun, we will not last. Get the staff together and have a ball!

10

"As Those Who Will Give an Account"
Maintaining a Heart for the Senior Pastor

"Obey your leaders, and submit to them; for they keep watch over your souls, as those who will give an account. Let them do this with joy and not with grief, for this would be unprofitable for you" (Hebrews 13:17).

"First of all, then, I urge that entreaties and prayers, petitions and thanksgivings, be made on behalf of all men, for kings and all who are in authority, in order that we may lead a tranquil and quiet life in all godliness and dignity" (1 Timothy 2:1-2).

The word *war* has received a lot of press lately. We have heard of "Star Wars" and "Airfare Wars," and, in reference to the scandals that rocked the church in 1987 and 1988, news commentators mockingly reported on "Holy Wars."

Holy wars, unfortunately, have never been limited to mega-ministries. Many have been fought within the ranks of the local church. Have you ever been involved in one? As a seminary student, I can vividly remember living through a church split. On Sunday, the congregation came together around the Lord's Supper and shared hymn books as they sang, "Blest Be the Tie That Binds." During the Wednesday-night business meeting, these same people threw those same hymn books at one another. I recall walking out of the meeting with tears streaming down my face. I considered leaving the ministry forever. Holy wars always leave deeply scarred and sometimes fatally wounded casualties in their wake.

Allow me to relate to you a priceless principle that I learned early on in the ministry: a divided staff will always result in a divided church. You will find no more important relationship in all of your ministry than the one between you and your senior pastor.

I have been deeply distressed at the number of youth workers, both lay and professional, who have told me that they and their senior pastors have locked horns in battle. I can remember as a young staff intern sitting in a staff meeting and watching in utter horror as the pastor and youth pastor shouted at each other. No wonder the church eventually split! In yet another church, a volunteer youth leader sowed such seeds of disloyalty toward the senior pastor that the youth group *en masse* pulled out of the church, crippling the integrity of the youth ministry for years. A divided staff will always result in a divided church.

FACTORS IN POOR STAFF RELATIONSHIPS

Pastoral staff relationships will always be fragile at best. They can break very easily, despite the high level of spiritual maturity we assume among those who serve together in ministry. Why does the relationship between a pastor and the staff break down?

Satan's strategy has always been to divide and conquer. Satan knows that if he can drive a wedge into a pastoral staff, he will have inflicted a potentially fatal blow, causing enormous damage to the church and ultimately to the reputation and program of God.

Some pastors feel threatened by the youth worker. Any staff member worth his salt will eventually attract a following. This happened in Corinth (" 'I am of Paul,' and 'I of Apollos,' and 'I of Cephas,' " 1 Corinthians 1:12) and, tragically, this happens today. Youth workers typically exude charisma and personality, and many have multiple gifts and talents, all of which can intimidate an insecure pastor.

Youth workers often communicate an independent spirit while chafing under the authority of the senior pastor. When two influential leaders head in opposite directions, it won't take much for that division to manifest itself.

Communication between the pastor and staff may break down. Every person on any level of spiritual leadership within a local church must understand the vision, directions, and goals of the senior pastor, and must be willing to support them wholeheartedly. This dynamic will never take place unless the pastor knows where he's going, knows why he is going there, and has clearly communicated this to the church as a whole and to the leaders in particular.

Petty differences will often occur among those in leadership. If left unresolved, such differences may eventually fester and grow into major resentments and bitterness.

Sometimes we do not allow one another to fail or to make mistakes. When we see someone we deeply respect fall flat on his face, a moment of truth has come. Disillusionment can set in. A harmonious relationship will result only when each person willingly allows the other to fail, consistently exhibiting an unconditional commitment to an imperfect person.

As we discuss the dynamics that make pastoral relationships work, let me first tell you where I am coming from. I have been involved in one local church youth ministry for more than ten years, ministering side by side with the same pastor. We have experienced a tremendous working relationship and a very deep and enduring friendship. I would be untruthful if I denied that at times our friendship was pushed to the limit. I did some pretty foolish things that got on his nerves and drove him up a wall. At times he hurt or disappointed me. Through much hard work coupled with an unconditional commitment to each other, we resolved a number of situations. I kept track of the lessons I learned during those years and will detail them for you in this chapter. My goal for these pages will have been accomplished if the relationships between a senior pastor and the members of his church's youth staff become stronger and grow deeper.

PRINCIPLES FOR A HEALTHY RELATIONSHIP

How does a youth worker maintain a heart for the senior pastor? Consider these seven principles.

1. Realize that the senior pastor is totally depraved.

I've got some bad news for you: so are you. Try this one on for size: so am I. None of us can claim exemption from depravity. Are you ready for a profound reality? "People are people." And people fail. Pastors fail. They make mistakes in judgment, say insensitive things, operate from less than noble motives, lose their tempers, and wound and offend people, sometimes without even knowing it. Once we come to grips with this reality, a lot of our unreal expectations will dissipate, and we will become less susceptible to disillusionment when we see our pastor blow it.

Check out Acts 15. Paul and Barnabas (we're talking relatively mature people here) had a major dispute. John Mark bailed out under pressure. Barnabas wanted to give Mark another chance; Paul wanted nothing to do with him. "There arose such a sharp disagreement that they separated from one another, and Barnabas took Mark with him and sailed away to Cyprus. But Paul chose Silas and departed" (Acts 15:39-40). The issue remained unresolved.

In another situation, Peter folded like a house of cards. "But when Cephas (Peter) came to Antioch, I opposed him to his face, because he stood condemned" (Galatians 2:11). He withdrew from eating with Gentiles because he feared ridicule and rejection. He gave in to sheer, unadulterated compromise. If Paul, Barnabas, and Peter can fall flat on their faces, dare we impose on our own pastors a higher expectation for their behavior?

Pastors are just people, and people are totally depraved. Perhaps we shouldn't be so surprised when our pastors blow it; perhaps we should be surprised that they don't blow it more often.

2. Remember that God always works His plan through the proper lines of authority.

As a youth pastor, I had to resolve the fact clearly in my mind that

God placed me under the authority of my senior pastor. He has the ultimate responsibility for the oversight of the church, and he will give an account for the ministry of the church as a whole—an enormous responsibility to say the least! I am on his staff; he is not on mine. I must, therefore, act in harmony with the direction the pastor has set for the church. Any deliberate violation of the pastor's expressed desire for the church would constitute an act of rebellion.

A disagreement with the overall direction of the church does not constitute a justifiable reason to rebel. God has always worked His plan through divinely constituted authority, even when the one in charge has been wrong. Paul showed proper respect for the high priest, even though that man represented a fallacious religious system (Acts 23:2-5). David knew that God had selected him as the next king. Saul had been plotting the murder of David for days. When given a perfect opportunity to kill Saul, David responded, "Do not destroy him, for who can stretch out his hand against the Lord's anointed and be without guilt?" (1 Samuel 26:9)

Leaders make mistakes. Yet our God can use even the mistakes of the one in authority to accomplish His plans and purposes. No man will ever stand in the way of God. God can remove him, change his heart, or allow the wrong course of action to eventually produce His desired results. If God can cause the wrath of men to praise Him, He can certainly handle an imperfect pastor. Don't you agree?

3. Understand that God often uses one under authority to change the heart of the one in authority.

Have you ever noticed that God often elevates His choicest servants to the position of number two rather than number one? God did not raise Joseph to the place of Pharaoh; He made Joseph second in command next to Pharaoh. Nehemiah did not hold the position of the king; he did become the cupbearer to the king. Daniel never ruled over Babylon; God placed him next to both Nebuchadnezzar and Darius, the men who did govern Babylon. Esther held the strategic place of influence over King Ahasuerus. Likewise, the youth pastor potentially holds a very strategic place of influence in the life of his senior pastor.

Such a prominent privilege, however, must be earned. No staff

MAINTAINING COMMUNICATION ON A TIGHT SCHEDULE

- Meet your pastor for breakfast one morning each week before you head off to work. Since both of you must eat, why not combine a meal with ministry?
- Phone your pastor at a given time each week to find out what he's got going and offer to pray for him.
- Does your pastor attend any seminars or conferences? The most meaningful times with my pastor resulted from my "tagging along" as he attended denominational meetings or pastors' conferences.
- What kind of hobbies is he into? Can you take him to a ball game? How about racquetball? You can discover a lot about the heart of a man by sitting with him in a golf cart in between holes.
- Can you arrange to run some errands with your pastor? I'll never forget the day my pastor invited me to meet him en route to a radio station while he dropped off some master tapes. We arranged the trip at a time that fit into both of our schedules, and we ended up "killing two birds with one stone."
- Do household projects together. Oh, the stories we could tell. One day the pastor came over to help me with my plumbing. He and I are big on creativity and short on patience. So naturally, we got right to it. He twisted the pipe wrench, splintered the pipe, and flooded my bathroom! Sometimes the best relationships are formed over the most bizarre shared experiences.
- Set a realistic goal. You don't need to meet weekly. Monthly, quarterly, or semiannual meetings will produce far greater results than no meetings at all.

person, whether full-time or part-time, paid or volunteer, will ever "get the ear" of the pastor without first demonstrating an unquestioned loyalty and an obvious sensitivity to biblical truth. Those who chafe under authority will rarely be elevated. Influence as a privilege must be earned, never demanded, and this will take time.

4. Diligently discern the dreams, visions, goals, and plans of the senior pastor for the church, and align yourself wholeheartedly behind them.

Let's hear it for the staff meeting! I know, I know—I hate meetings too. But the weekly staff meeting should prove the exception. The staff meeting provides the best forum in which regular, heart-to-heart communication can take place. The pastor and his staff can talk through the present condition of the entire church body while setting a direction and determining the course of action to get there. This should be a meeting of minds and hearts as each one visualizes the potential of what God can accomplish through the various ministries of the church. Each meeting should be positive, productive, and problem-solving in nature. Each staff member should be supported and affirmed by the others.

The key to communication will always remain a constant: time. Unfortunately, time may be hard to come by, especially if you as the leader of the youth ministry find your employment outside of the church.

Meaningful communication can take place with a minimum commitment of time when these two prerequisites hold true: (1) you understand the vital importance of regular communication with your pastor, and (2) he has a heartfelt commitment to the vital importance of youth ministry.

As our pastors' goals and direction become clear, we youth pastors have the unique opportunity of demonstrating our loyalty by becoming excited about helping the pastor to fulfill his goals in any way possible. The highest calling of the youth pastor is to make the pastor as effective as possible. We should not seek to build only the youth ministry, but to enhance and supplement the ministry of the senior pastor. Youth ministry will thrive only in a church that is healthy overall.

While the goal of our communication will always center on our desire for a harmonious, like-minded relationship, disagreements and differences of opinions will occur. These need not be viewed as negative sitations. The decisions of one leader most often result from the input of his many advisors. A variety of viewpoints should prove as valuable to a church staff as the octave of notes is to a musician. Unfortunately, an improper arrangement will always produce discord rather than harmony.

What should you as a youth worker do when you adamantly disagree with the pastor? You must ask yourself, "Does this issue constitute a nonnegotiable? Does this violate a biblical conviction I would refuse to compromise no matter what the cost?"

A friend of mine was told by his board that he could no longer allow unsaved teenagers to attend any activities or Bible studies. "We are afraid they will want to date our daughters." I don't know about you, but for me that would constitute a nonnegotiable.

I can remember wanting to have a parents' meeting in the local Elks' Lodge since unsaved parents would more likely come to a neutral meeting place. The pastor adamantly refused. This did not constitute for me a nonnegotiable issue. This was merely my preference.

You can appeal a decision with which you do not agree. Daniel 1 clearly illustrates this principle. Daniel respectfully requested an alternate plan based on the wishes of the king. After carefully wording his request, Daniel trusted God to express His will through the one in authority.

If the appeal is refused, demonstrate flexibility concerning your preferences. If the issue falls into the category of a nonnegotiable (and these will be extremely rare, involving the violation of a clear biblical absolute), you have no alternative but to resign. If you don't, the first steps toward a church split will have been taken.

You may now be thinking, "Where, then, do my goals fit in? At what point do I begin to lay out my plans for the youth ministry?"

5. Acknowledge both your boundaries and your freedom.

We have two boundaries. We can do whatever we want as long as we do not violate a biblical absolute or run counter to the direction of the church as set by the pastor.

We have tremendous freedom. Do you want to spend time on public school campuses? Do it. Do you want to set up service projects in your community? Do it. How about a mission trip during Easter week? Go for it. Have you ever thought of establishing an outreach to latchkey kids, staffed and funded by your young people? Set it up. Dream your dreams, mobilize your students, and change the world! Too much of the time we dwell on what we cannot do rather than becoming excited about what we can do.

BUILDING TRUST WITH THE BOARD

You must understand how board members think. Some take themselves far too seriously, having convinced themselves that they are the watchdogs for the kingdom. Others have the same concern we have for reaching youth but do not know how to go about it; they need to be educated regarding present-day youth culture. The majority understand their role very clearly and would die for you and me. This third group you will never need to worry about. The second group will come around the more they sense your heart. The first group you will need to tolerate and avoid as much as possible. Treat them with respect because they are on the board. Answer their questions as clearly as possible, never giving more information than is requested. Listen politely and with a teachable spirit to their suggestions. Then continue on in your ministry. When challenged, view this as a positive opportunity to further train the board in youth ministry while rallying them to your side, rather than as a negative threat to your ministry. A godly response of respect and humility will go a long way toward building trust.

At this point, I need to add a vitally important perspective. The pastor and the board too have responsibilities for making the staff relationship work. They need to understand that once they have invited an individual to join the church staff, they have, in essence, given him full endorsement to do whatever he feels he must do in overseeing the youth ministry of the church. A call must be accompanied by a great amount of trust. The pastor and his board must give the youth pastor as much latitude as possible to do the job they have called him to do. Any board who calls someone only to place him in a straitjacket does the work of the Lord an unthinkable disservice.

The purpose of the church board is to provide the support that is needed to guarantee a staff member's success; it is never to flaunt its authority, reducing him to a mere pawn in their hands. A youth pastor has not been hired by the church to carry out the whims and wishes of the board or the pastor. He has been called by God to carry out the will of God in reaching the youth of his city. "Oh, but we pay his salary. He works for us." No, he doesn't. The church provides his support; it does not pay his salary. A matter of semantics, you ask? "Salary" implies an employer–employee relationship. The board becomes the employer as it pays its employee to do its bidding. "Support" suggests that God has commissioned the staff member to give his full time in serving the youth of his city. By taking up his support, the church allows the staff member to do what God has called him to do without the encumbrance of other full-time employment.

My advice to church board members has always been the same. As long as the youth pastor does not violate a biblical absolute (we're not talking about the personal preferences of the people on the board!) and does not run counter to the direction of the church ministry as a whole, *leave him alone.*

The average tenure of a youth pastor today varies between nine and eighteen months, depending upon the survey. One reason for the untimely demise of the youth pastor, given far too frequently, is that the church board ate him alive! God forbid this should ever happen in your situation.

6. Refuse to hear a person's criticism of the pastor. Yes, gossip can be completely eliminated. Sound impossible? Check this out: when someone comes to you for the expressed purpose of criticizing another staff member, refuse to hear him. Politely but firmly state, "I am sorry but I really do not want, nor do I need, to hear what you are saying. He is my friend and I stand with him in absolute loyalty."

Second, insist that the person go to the pastor to express his concerns with him face-to-face. The person obviously felt the seriousness of the situation justified his coming to you; therefore, it is serious enough for him to go to the pastor.

And then the kicker: tell the critic that you will be informing the pastor that he will be coming to see him with a serious concern within the week. You might add that if he doesn't make contact within the week, the pastor will be calling him.

Needless to say, the disgruntled critic feels stunned. We follow through. Each of us on staff holds the identical commitment to each other. Gossip immediately stops. Our heartfelt commitment to one another becomes the pattern for the church body as a whole.

7. Deal with offenses as quickly as possible.
Relationships will always be dynamic, never static. They require a constant effort to maintain. Too often, major breakdowns occur as the result of a series of "little offenses" that were never resolved.

I would suggest this basic guideline: If something is big enough to hurt, it is big enough to heal. How can this be accomplished?

When an offense occurs, sit down as quickly as possible and honestly reveal your feelings. Assume the best. Rarely in a staff relationship will one member deliberately try to hurt another. Simply express, without projecting blame or a judgmental attitude, "When you said this, I was hurt. Let me tell you why. . . . " Regardless of the other's response, forgive (Matthew 18:21-22).

When you hurt another, ask for forgiveness. So often we have the attitude, "But what about what he did to me? I'll ask his forgiveness only after he asks mine." I have a little sign in my office that has helped me tremendously: "I am not afraid to go first." Get the point? I am responsible before God to do what I know I must, regardless of the other person's response. Jesus said, "If therefore you are presenting your offering at the altar, and there remember that your brother has something against you, leave your offering there before the altar, and go your way; first be reconciled to your brother, and then come and present your offering" (Matthew 5:23-24).

After resolving a situation, drop it. Love "does not take into account a wrong suffered" (1 Corinthians 13:5). Forgiveness can be defined as "wiping the slate clean" (an application of Ephesians 4:32). Allow the slate of your memory to remain clean.

Determine that this process will be followed every time the situation calls for resolution.

"A divided staff will always result in a divided church." Satan has had a heyday in discrediting ministries over petty, insignificant differences that spread like gangrene throughout the church body. The best safeguard against such an attack will be a selfless commitment to seeking the very best for the other person as we do all we can to make our pastors effective. When this heart attitude becomes characteristic of us, then we will have taken the first steps toward harmonious, long-term relationships with our senior pastors.

CHECKING YOUR HEART:
A Personal EKG

1. Take a sheet of paper and describe in fifty words or less your present relationship with your senior pastor. Is it everything you want it to be? What changes would you make if you had the power to do so? Has he been made aware that you feel this way? Have you considered taking him out to lunch and sharing with him honestly and openly how you feel?

2. List some positive ways in which you have recently communicated to your pastor your love, respect, and loyalty. Do you drop him little notes of encouragement on occasion? Women, have you made an effort to encourage his wife? Ministry can be relentlessly lonely and discouraging. You will never know the value of an encouraging word until you have walked in his shoes. Why not set as a goal a personal expression of your undying support on a monthly basis? Formulate a list of creative ways in which this can be done:

- a phone call in which you ask him what you can pray for;
- a note in which you thank him for a specific insight you received from a sermon;
- send him a book that you found especially stimulating to your own faith;
- clip out an article he might use as an illustration;
- befriend his children;
- send birthday and anniversary cards;
- leave a note on the pulpit in which you simply state, "I'm praying for you this morning";
- sit near the front of the church and take notes during the sermon;
- if you have any platform responsibilities, refer to the blessing the pastor has been in your life;
- never criticize him but purpose in your heart to speak only positively about him to others.

These are only the beginning. You come up with your own.

3. Can you define the direction the pastor has set for the church? Describe his philosophy of ministry. What does he want the church to look like in five years? Ten years? How does he evaluate success? How does the youth ministry fit with all of this? If you cannot answer these questions with any sense of certainty, you'd better find out. There is only one place to find the answers.

What about your goals for the youth ministry? Where are you headed? What do you want your ministry to look like in the next five years? Ten years? Does your ministry direction flow with his? Are you complementing the pastor or competing with him? Do you see any potential conflicts? Have you and the pastor discussed this?

4. List your pastor's strengths and weaknesses. Now list yours. Can you visualize ways in which you can complement the ministry of your pastor? By understanding his weaknesses, can you now better tolerate situations in which his weaknesses show through? Have you been guilty of placing your pastor on a pedestal by not allowing him to be a human being? Have you overreacted whenever certain weaknesses have expressed themselves? Do you regularly pray for your pastor in relation to these weaknesses, or have you allowed yourself to become bitter?

5. Are you experiencing any conflicts with the board? When you read my comments directed at the board, did you feel tempted to say, "Preach it, brother"? If so, might I suggest that you discuss this chapter with your pastor? Tread lightly. Don't militantly march into a board meeting waving this book while declaring war.

6. Every youth staff person should do a personal study of 1 Corinthians 13:4-7, Matthew 18:21-35, Romans 12:16-21, and 1 Peter 2:13-25. These passages form the basis for a study on the subjects of love, forgiveness, bitterness, and submission toward authority. After your study, determine if you are bitter toward anyone who has deeply hurt or offended you, particularly your pastor. What steps will you take to resolve the problem?

7. Reread the parable in Matthew 18:23-35. Christ's forgiveness of us forms the basis of our ability to forgive one another. Make a list of everything the person did to deeply hurt or offend you. Do not overlook a thing. Next, list all of the things you did to offend God. The one slave experienced the forgiveness of a $10 million debt ("ten thousand talents"). Christ has forgiven us of a $10 million debt (your second list). Yet, this same slave would not forgive a fellow slave of an $18 debt. Unthinkable. Having been forgiven of a $10 million debt, cannot we forgive another of an $18 debt (our first list)?

8. Finally, make a list of every possible benefit that has come to your life through the painful situation you experienced. Give this some thought. God certainly allowed the situation for a reason. What was it? How has this situation benefited your life? "In everything [even painful things] give thanks; for this is God's will for you in Christ Jesus" (1 Thessalonians 5:18). How can we develop a thankful heart even in the midst of personal pain? By recognizing the positive benefits that will result in our lives through our painful experiences.

11

"Do All to the Glory of God"
Maintaining a Heart for Excellence in Activity Planning

"Whatever your hand finds to do, verily, do it with all your might" (Ecclesiastes 9:10).

"Can you describe your most embarrassing moment?" The question came from a guy sitting in the back row of the chapel, and 600 pairs of eyeballs were riveted on me, excitedly awaiting my answer. My mind began to spin like a floppy disk, my life flashing through my frontal lobes. I thought of so many experiences. I remembered getting kicked out of the "Howdy Doody Show" for being too rowdy. I recalled playing hide-and-seek in K-Mart and thinking my friend had hidden in a dressing room. I suddenly pulled back the dressing room curtain while shouting at the top of my voice, "I got you!" only to discover a stark naked man trying on a bathing suit! I thought of some others as well. . . .

My mind painfully returned to my Beach Barbeque Wienie Roast. I had this thing organized to the hilt. Huntington Beach! Incredibly beautiful day! One hundred fifty high school kids! Waves! Surfboards! Food for an army! Charcoal! Buns and beans! Ketchup and mustard! Hangers on which to barbeque the hot dogs! I mean I had it all! With one fatal exception—I had forgotten a can opener! We had to use the church bus oil spout to pour the beans into the pan. The kids never knew it, but several told me the beans were the tastiest they had ever eaten!

How about our "Bigger and Better Party"? Simple enough. Divide everybody into teams. Give them a toothpick. Tell them to go door to door, trading the toothpick for something bigger or better. I gave the kids two hours. The team with the biggest or best item would win. Couldn't be easier, right? The winning team rode into the church sanctuary on a horse! Another team carried back an unused World War II torpedo! That's what happens when you omit one little rule—I had forgotten to tell them they had to keep whatever they brought back!

How about the car rally in which more than 100 students ended up at Ida Wong's house? The problem? None of us knew Ida Wong. It's amazing what can happen when the opening clue contains a slight inaccuracy.

My tales of woe could continue. I won't take the time to tell you about the night a homeowner pulled a shotgun on the pastor's son, or the night my entire youth group forcibly sat through a lecture on bells. (Bells? Bells! Three hundred bells, including their country of origin and distinguishing characteristics!) I have some memories just too painful to tell.

Every youth worker will plan his fair share of activities. The number of details can be enormous and the unexpected can be bizarre. I have done activity programming for groups ranging in size from 5 to over 400. Can we oversee activities while maintaining a semblance of sanity? That's what this chapter is all about.

QUALITY OVER QUANTITY

As we begin, allow me to make two assumptions. First, the planning of activities can be easily delegated to members of the lay staff. A theological education is not a prerequisite. Anyone who possesses a heart for meeting the specific needs of young people, coupled with a semblance of organizational ability, will do just fine by following the step-by-step approach in this chapter.

Second, activity planning does not hold the top spot on your list of priorities. Too many youth pastors have been reduced to glorified activity directors. Many of my friends have become frustrated and burned out while trying to maintain an activity calendar that would make the head of a whirling dervish spin. Activities are an extremely important dimension of youth ministry, but not the most important. You can have the best planned and executed activities in the world but score a zero on spiritual impact.

What's the point? Just this: Your priorities will dictate the frequency of activities but never their quality. If, after having established your ministry priorities, you determine that you must give the bulk of your time to other dimensions of ministry, cut back on the number of activities. But do not cut back on their quality. Determine that you would rather plan fewer activities with excellence than many with mediocrity.

Everything we do from Bible studies to pizza pig-outs must demonstrate our commitment to quality. Anything less will only communicate to our students the perception that Christianity is a two-bit, second-rate, low-budget religion. Oh, I know it's a cliché, but it's so true: God gave us His best. Can we do anything less? Ours must be the commitment of David—he would not give God anything that cost him nothing (2 Samuel 24:24).

A STEP-BY-STEP GUIDE TO ACTIVITY PLANNING

With that as a brief introduction, let's turn our attention to the principles that make activity planning a rich and rewarding reality.

The following agenda will work for the most complex activities. We will not need to follow every step every time. Obviously, a swim party for 15 will require a whole lot less planning than a five-day water-ski trip for 200. Simply take this list and adapt it for your own needs.

1. Establish a clearly defined purpose for every activity.

The failure to establish a purpose for every activity constitutes one of the most common fatal flaws in youth ministry. Never do anything without meaning. Why? Three reasons. One, we don't have time to waste. Two, we do not want to produce an activity-oriented group of students; we do want to produce an achievement-oriented group. Activities represent expenditures of time with nothing lasting to show for them. Achievement requires clearly defined, worthwhile, and lasting goals. Three, every staff person possesses an inherent need to feel significant. Significance results from an investment of time producing meaningful results rather than from a waste of time producing no lasting results.

The youth staff should consider the question "What needs do I sense within our young people that can best be met through the use of a social activity?" Luke 2:52 chronicles for us the four general categories of human need: Jesus increased in wisdom, (mental needs), in stature (physical needs), and in favor with God (spiritual needs) and men (social needs). Consider this partial list of possible needs within a youth group:

- The fostering of deeper friendships among the young people within the group, especially during times of rapid growth, when cliques have become a major problem, or when several schools are represented within the ministry.
- The provision of a hands-on opportunity for the students to share their faith with their unsaved friends.
- The creation of a nonthreatening environment to which the students can invite their friends who may never consider darkening the door of a church.
- The formation of a service project during which our commitment to serving one another, our neighbors, or the community as a whole can be reinforced.
- The exposure of students to a cross-cultural missions environment.

- The raising of money for an upcoming camp, missions need, or church-wide project.
- The enhancement of group unity through a shared experience.
- The provision of some good, clean, wholesome fun.

Once you have compiled this list of needs as a staff, you can take the second step.

2. Choose the activities based on the purpose. Do nothing without meaning.

If my staff determined that the young people needed an opportunity to invite their unsaved friends to a nonthreatening environment, we would not take them to the park to pass out tracts. We might, however, play Capture the Flag in the park. If we wanted to encourage group unity by forcing the students out of their cliques, we would not take them to Disneyland; the moment the bus hit the parking lot, they would grab their friends and go. We might plan a car rally, have the teenagers place their names on slips of paper when they arrive, and randomly draw the names out of a hat, five to a car. You can be sure that new friendships will be built as they work on solving the clues together.

WHAT ABOUT DEVOTIONS?

Must every event end with devotions? An event should include devotions only when the goals of the event call for them. If you have set up a fund-raising event, why have devotions? If you have created an atmosphere in which new friendships can be formed, why include devotions unless they are germane to the purposes behind the activity? If you have set up a service project, you might want to rally the students together before they hit the streets and give them a ten-minute shot about the need to serve one another.

Our students should be hearing solidly biblical messages in our regular Bible studies, not to mention the sermons they hear in church. That is ample truth for anyone to assimilate in one week without throwing devotions into the middle of a skate night, don't you think?

By establishing the purposes first and choosing activities based on the purposes, the following will result: you and the entire staff will feel a sense of achievement as you meet the clearly defined goals; you will experience the thrill of meeting specific needs in the lives of the young people; the young people will learn to discern and model our achievement orientation as they see a goal accomplished; the activity calendar will have a sense of balance since every event centers on a comprehensive list of purposes; you will have avoided the leading cause of youth ministry burnout—the expenditure of time and energy with nothing lasting to show for it; you will be following the most important programming priority: DO NOTHING WITHOUT MEANING.

Let me throw in a philosophical note at this point. "Creating a Christian alternative" does not express a valid purpose for a special event. We have not been called by God to compete with the world. We wouldn't be able to, even if we wished. Jesus prayed in John 17 not that His Father would take the disciples out of the world, but that He would protect them from the evil one. You will run yourself ragged if you live under the illusion that the church is responsible to "get the kids off the street." Let me say it loud and clear: the parents have the responsibility of getting their kids off the street, not the church and certainly not you.

As a youth pastor, I have consistently motivated my students to get involved in as many wholesome school activities as possible. I encourage them to run for office, play sports, join the drama team, become cheerleaders, or whatever. These involvements will provide our young people with the opportunities they need to form a network of relationships through which the Gospel can flow. They will never win the world if we don't encourage them to have any unsaved friends.

One vivid example stands out clearly in my mind. A mother called me to find out what I had planned for prom night so that her daughter wouldn't go to the prom. She just about popped her appendix when I told her that I had planned nothing for prom night. I am certainly not foolish enough to think that I can compete with the senior prom. And I gently informed her that if she didn't want her daughter to go, she, not I, was responsible to tell her.

So how did I deal with the prom? In my city, the proms had traditionally been very dangerous events. I formulated a three-point plan: prepare the students by teaching them the potential evil associated with the prom; encourage staff members to offer their services as chaperones at the prom (their presence will clearly communicate their love for and commitment to the students, while silently motivating them to resist harmful behavior); and work through any student officers in the group to gain a positive influence in the planning of the prom.

One year we had the senior class president, student body vice president, treasurer, and social coordinator in our group. I met with them, and together we planned the prom—everything from food to music. The principal called me after the prom to thank me for my influence as he informed me that the prom was the most wholesome he could remember! That would not have been possible if I had tried to plan a "Christian alternative" to the prom.

3. Include a committee in the planning, promoting, and executing of each activity.

What's that old line? "A mule is a horse put together by a committee." I'll tell you right now—I'm not big on committees. The planning, promotion, and execution of activities, however, is my one major exception. Let me tell you why.

A committee will help share the load. Considering the number of details to which attention must be given, the administration of each event will prove much more effective when several people shoulder the responsibilities.

An involvement of a number of people will produce a pooled creativity. One good brainstorming session can save hours of futile thinking by just one individual.

Each committee member will have ownership of each event. They will work hard to produce an activity of excellence since it is theirs.

An infectious enthusiasm for each event will spread throughout the group, generated by those who have been in on things from the very beginning.

A committee will provide a pool of resources. What do you need for your next social? Ski boats? Swimming pools? Volleyballs? Split the list among committee members and see what they come up with.

Where do the members come from? The social committee should

AFFIRM EVERY HELPER

Everyone needs to feel significant. Everyone wants to know that God used him or her to accomplish something meaningful in the lives of someone else. A thank-you note sent to every helper a week after the activity will reinforce a sense of significance.

Include the following in your note:

- a restatement of the goals for the activity;
- specific mention of the role the person played in helping to achieve the goals;
- an expression of the positive benefits that came to the group as a whole or to individuals in particular because of the person's involvement in the activity;
- personal appreciation for the privilege of working with such a quality individual.

Think about this: If you had sacrificed hours of personal time to plan and pull off a youth activity, wouldn't a note like this make you feel like you invested your time wisely? Wouldn't such a note motivate you to want to get involved in future activities?

consist of the lay staff, a few key young people (by *key,* I mean students who have shown themselves faithful and who also understand the likes and dislikes of the broad cross-section of students at their schools), and interested parents who understand the needs of today's young people.

4. Schedule early to avoid conflicts.

Spare yourself the embarrassment I have had to endure far too many times. The cliché certainly applies to our ministries: "First come, first served." I once had to cancel an activity for 100 students because 10 people in our deaf group had reserved the facility for the same evening.

Anything requiring reservations must be done as far in advance as possible. Consider the following: rooms, equipment, buses, drivers, fields, camps, parks, the church kitchen, sound systems, etc. Commit yourself to the goal of making every reservation within one week of your planning meeting. If you don't, you may find yourself and your young people literally standing out in the cold.

5. Investigate all facilities ahead of time.

Take nothing for granted. We cannot rely on promotional materials since they typically picture only the best corner of the facility. We cannot operate solely on a friend's recommendation since people's perceptions differ.

I once paid dearly for violating this principle. We planned a weekend retreat for seventy-five high school students. I spoke personally to the director of the camp and told him of our need for a field. He assured me that he had one available that would more than adequately meet our needs. All of our programming for the weekend depended on the availability of that field. When we arrived, I found out to my horror that the field was located in the bottom of a canyon, three quarters of a mile straight down from the main camp. Snow blanketed the camp, rendering the field totally inaccessible.

Facilities must be checked out by those who will be responsible for the programming of the event. Such a precaution will eliminate all surprises while allowing for the maximum use of the facility.

6. Make a list of every conceivable detail and delegate to members of the committee.

This list must be comprehensive and detailed. No matter how insignificant an item may seem, place it on the list.

Don't just write "promotion." What kind of promotion? Phone calling? Printed fliers? Announcements? Skits? When will the promotion take place? Will fliers be sent one week before the event? A month before? Three months before? How many fliers will be sent? Just one? One and then a follow-up? Who will design them? How many will you need?

Do you need to include a map or directions? Can the students drive, or will they need transportation? How about food? Athletic equipment? Song sheets? Bullhorns? First-aid kits? Medical release forms? (An absolute must! A doctor will not treat an injured person without one.) Who will stay late in the church parking lot until the parents pick up the last student? Who will clean up after the event ends?

Once the list has been completed, each item should be delegated to a member of the committee. One week before the activity, the one in charge of the event should call those to whom responsibilities have been delegated in order to make sure that every base has been covered. Once the social takes place, it's a little late to discover that someone dropped the ball.

7. Meet with the committee one half hour before the event.

The more complex the activity, the more necessary this becomes. Why a meeting?

The one in charge can remind the staff of the purposes of the social. This promotes unity among the staff as each one strives for the same goals.

The order of events within the activity itself can be reviewed.

Any last minute questions can be answered.

A quick review just before the activity begins will guarantee that every base has indeed been covered with nothing of significance overlooked.

The staff can pray together, asking God to accomplish His purposes.

An early meeting will assure that no adults arrive late. We should always commit ourselves to the goal of beginning on time and ending on time. Late arrivals paralyze us at this point.

8. Count on it: something unforeseen will go wrong.

I could tell you stories that would curl your hair. We've had injuries. We've had kids lost. We've had young people get sick. We've had buses break down. These things will happen; they are inevitable.

Over the years, experience has proven that the unexpected experiences provide the greatest teaching opportunities and the best memories. The students who face such situations can always benefit as they watch their leaders creatively handle pressure situations.

While such problems can prove profitable in the long run, they must never result from bad planning. The young people and their parents will accept the fact that things go wrong unless we caused the situations by a careless oversight.

9. Meet together a week or two after the activity for evaluation.

No activity will be complete without this step. The evaluation process does not require much time, but it must be done. As a committee, review these questions:

- Did we achieve the goals we set out to accomplish? If not, why not?
- Should we run this activity again in the future?
- Could this event have been more effective? If so, how?
- Was this event done with excellence? If not, what should we change?
- What caught us by surprise? What should we have anticipated that we didn't?

10. Remember, carry out a few activities with excellence rather than many with mediocrity.

Excellence is a mandate, not a preference. Whatever our hands find to do, we must do wholeheartedly, putting everything we've got into it (Ecclesiastes 9:10). Our God deserves nothing less; our young people deserve nothing less.

We don't have the time, obviously, to plan innumerable activities. Our students don't have time to participate in innumerable activities. A proper commitment to their families coupled with their involvement in school activities will easily eat up most of their time. *The only reason to plan a social activity is to meet the needs that can best be met through such an event.* Any other reason will prove illegitimate.

How many socials should you plan? The answer will be based on a number of factors: your assessed needs, the number of adult support staff, ministry goals and priorities, the number of school events, etc. In most cases, one activity every three weeks should prove sufficient.

And please remember that there is beauty in simplicity. Not every activity needs to become an administrative nightmare. Most young people simply love to get together, even when the event requires only a minimum of planning.

Let this dimension of ministry become fun rather than drudgery, meaningful rather than a waste. I sincerely hope that these principles will enhance your enjoyment of the planning and execution of social activities, ultimately resulting in the changed lives of your young people.

CHECKING YOUR HEART:
A Personal EKG

1. Take out your calendar. How many social events did you have in the last three months? Why did you have them? Can you remember the specific purposes for each one, or did you have any just for the sake of having them? Statements like "But we always have a Christmas banquet" do not adequately justify an event.

2. Who are the members of the social committee? Do you need to build one? Can you identify a few key students in the youth group who would help to keep you informed of the likes and dislikes of your group? Can you think of some parents who might not want the responsibilities of a full-fledged staff member but who might enjoy helping out with social activities?

3. List every need of the group you can think of. Which of the needs can best be met by a social activity? As a committee, begin to relate social events to the specific needs you all have identified.

4. Once the activities have been determined and the dates set, take a good look at the list and ask yourselves if your social calendar reflects balance. Remember that needs come in four categories: mental, physical, spiritual, and social. Students need to have fun but they also need to serve others. Through the youth ministry as a whole, are the comprehensive needs of the student being met? In a word, are your youth ministry in general and your social calendar in particular well-rounded?

5. Have some fun with promotion. Brainstorm this one and get as crazy as you want. Skits, fliers, mailings, public service announcements on local radio stations (they're free!), banners, and blurbs in the school bulletin can all be used effectively. Do not, however, send or do anything that isn't sharp looking. A second-rate flier will say more about the upcoming event than anything else on the paper. And make sure you include every detail. I recently received one flier announcing an event while omitting the date! Take nothing for granted. You cannot overcommunicate.

6. Draw up an activity planning sheet (a sample is included in Appendix H). This will serve as a helpful check list for the delegation of any activity.

7. Does each young person have a signed permission slip on file? You do not need a new slip for each event. They can be dated for a specified period of time and include all events within that time period. Whenever a young person expresses any interest in your youth group, pass along a permission slip. (Appendix I has one that you may copy.)

12

"Iron Sharpens Iron"
Maintaining a Heart for the Critic

"Iron sharpens iron, so one man sharpens another" (Proverbs 27:17).

"If possible, so far as it depends on you, be at peace with all men. Never take on your own revenge, beloved, but leave room for the wrath of God, for it is written, 'Vengeance is Mine, I will repay,' says the Lord. 'But if your enemy is hungry, feed him, and if he is thirsty, give him a drink; for in so doing you will heap burning coals upon his head.' Do not be overcome by evil, but overcome evil with good" (Romans 12:18-21).

Have you ever wanted to go back to bed and start the day over? Only about five times a week, right? I was in the grip of one of the worst days of my entire existence when the mail came and my secretary announced that I received a personal letter. "Here," she said, handing it to me, "this will cheer you up, I hope." I tore into the envelope with eager expectation and read these words:

> Dewey:
>
> Just a little note to inform you of how offended I was by your letter of May 11. It is unbelievable to me how a so-called "messenger of God" could be so callous. First of all, you keep sending me these ridiculous fliers and announcements when I haven't really been to church in six months. Then, the letter I do get from you (supposedly) is photocopied and headed "Hey, my friend." Friend? My God, Dewey, you haven't even taken the time to say more than hello to me in six months! If all my friends were like you, I'm sure I'd spend many crying, lonely nights with no one to talk to.
>
> Then your letter goes on to say "how much I appreciate you!" Appreciate me so much that in six months you haven't been able to drop me a note addressed to me and not to 100 kids you couldn't care less about? I don't ask love or appreciation from you, Dewey, but I will gladly accept it if it is truly meant and from the heart. Otherwise, DON'T BOTHER.
>
> Do you even know or care what has happened in my life since October? I don't think so. Our wonderful "youth pastor" only cares about his own little cliques—can this be possible? I would suggest that you reach out a little more and then maybe you wouldn't lose so many Christians in need of love to Satan.
>
> Not that I believe in Satan. I don't even believe in God anymore. And I'm happy because even without some "happily ever after" God I can still find beauty in a flower. I live to make sure my friends are happy and I see to it that they don't get form letters or pre-written speeches when they are in need of help. Sometimes I feel sorry for you fairy-tale Christians. I don't think you really live in reality. The world contains many horrible things (as I have found out lately). But I have accepted the world as it is and can now live in peace with it. Not that I am sinless—far from it. But even living among the

horrible things and doing "evil" things is better than standing above the world looking down.

I feel very sad, Dewey, because my opinion of you has really fallen since November. You strike me as a hypocrite who preaches brotherly love and yet does not live it. And even if I wake up next Sunday morning in bed with another girl I will know our sins are equal in the sight of your God because I care enough about the people I love not to let them sit waiting for six months without a word from me.

I am very sorry, Dewey, but I have held this inside too long and had to tell you. I hope with all my heart that you will think about this. And even if you don't agree, still think long and hard.

Sincerely,
Julie

Just what I needed! Kick a man when he's down, right? I thought to myself, "Just let me go home and go back to bed!"

The entire situation described in the letter had begun innocently enough. I had photocopied a letter announcing an upcoming event and sent it to everyone on the mailing list. Julie (not her real name) would surely not expect me to send a handwritten, personal letter to everyone in the youth group every time we have a social, would she? It's certainly not my fault she left the group, is it? I can't be expected to notice every time someone doesn't show up at a Bible study, can I? And what's this stuff about losing "so many Christians in need of love to Satan," and "I don't believe in God anymore"? She even hinted at the possibility of perversion when she said, "even if I wake up next Sunday morning in bed with another girl," didn't she? "Consider the source," they used to tell me. Do I have to take such verbal abuse from an apostate lesbian?

I asked a friend what he thought, and he confirmed my thoughts. "Forget it, Dewey," he told me. "That letter doesn't even deserve a response." I promptly wadded it up, threw it out, and went about my business, still wishing I could go to bed and forget this day even happened. But I couldn't get Julie's words out of my mind. They cut very deeply and wounded me greatly. Do you know why? Because in the core of my being I knew that she was right.

Mark this well: Criticism, like the waves of the sea, will come crashing in upon you, one wave following another. Criticism goes with the territory. We will never succeed in pleasing all of the people all of the time.

LEARNING FROM CRITICISM

Why does God allow us to experience the vented wrath of someone's critical spirit? Isn't ministry draining enough without this kind of thing? Can we discern a divine purpose behind criticism? Consider these factors.

Criticism reveals our blind spots. You have yours and I have mine—areas of character deficiency that are visible to everyone except us. I have been both shocked and amazed at how easily I can, by a thoughtless word or harsh facial expression, literally devastate another person without ever realizing what I have done. Criticism provides us with a golden opportunity for self-examination through which we can discover more of our blind spots. Like the man said, "The truth hurts." But sometimes we need to take a good long look into a mirror, even when it causes us to say "Ouch!"

Criticism keeps us humble. Ever wonder how in the world the kingdom got along so well for so many years without you? I tend to forget sometimes that God can use rocks and even Balaam's ass if He wants. Whenever I begin looking for the next vacancy in the Trinity, I get hit in the face with harsh criticism.

Criticism reveals the needs of the critic. Criticism often results from deep, unresolved conflicts in the life of the critic. The letter with which I began serves as a classic example of a very troubled girl desperately crying out for help. The key phrase appears halfway through the letter: "I would suggest that you reach out a little more and then maybe you wouldn't lose so many Christians in need of love to Satan." Why don't you reread the letter and see how many additional clues Julie gives to the conflicts currently taking place in her personal life?

Criticism opens doors of ministry to hurting people. This letter demands a response. Most criticism does. When a person allows himself the luxury of taking a cheap shot at us, he concedes the possibility of granting us equal time. When we respond correctly, our credibility skyrockets in the eyes of our critics; when we respond incorrectly, the criticism will only remain confirmed.

Criticism teaches us the pain we cause others when we criticize them. The pain I felt when I read the letter is something I will not soon forget. Have harsh and insensitive words caused others the same hurt that I experienced? The importance of Ephesians 4:29—"Let no unwholesome word proceed from your mouth, but only such a word as is good for edification according to the need of the moment, that it may give grace to those who hear"—becomes underscored in my thinking every time I become subjected to someone's critical comments.

Criticism might result from a satanic attempt to discourage or defeat us. Discouragement, depression, and disillusionment provide a trio of very powerful arrows in Satan's quiver. He loves to plant in my mind thoughts like these: "I am useless. My life has accomplished nothing lasting. I have no fruit that has remained. I am a hypocrite because I continuously fail to live up to the standard I seek to set for others. I am hindering the work of God and should just give up and get out of the way." Do you ever entertain thoughts like these? Are they ever fueled by the malicious criticism you receive from others? If so, you have been handed a golden opportunity to defeat the enemy at the point of attack.

RESPONDING TO CRITICISM

So what's the answer? How should I properly respond to my critics? Ignore them? Prostrate myself before them? What should I do when I honestly believe that I have been victimized by unwarranted or unjustified criticism? The remainder of this chapter will detail the steps I took in response to the letter.

1. View criticism as a valuable opportunity rather than a negative situation.

This sounds so trite that I hesitate to mention it. Yet, we've got to start here. If we don't, criticism will eat us alive. If we view criticism in the negative, we will inevitably find ourselves in danger of quitting, compromising, lashing back, closing our lives off to the one who's hurt us, becoming bitter, vengeful, defensive, disillusioned, or defeated.

We properly respond to criticism when we thank God for it when it comes. Only then will God have the opportunity to accomplish in our lives the purposes for which He allowed the criticism in the first place. The writer of Hebrews summarizes this principle well: "See to it that no one comes short of the grace of God; that no root of bitterness springing up causes trouble, and by it many be defiled" (Hebrews 12:15).

2. Evaluate yourself.

Has the critic identified a blind spot that until now went unnoticed in my life? In the case of my letter, the answer was a resounding yes. Let's go through the letter and let me show you what I mean.

Julie questioned how "a so-called 'messenger of God' could be so callous." I communicated callousness by neglecting a girl in my youth group for six months—the most critical, difficult six months in her life. I found out later that she was experiencing monumental conflicts both in her family and in her personal life to the point of renouncing her faith while turning to lesbianism. I called myself her pastor. And yet, during the most traumatic six months of her life, I hadn't even noticed that she was missing. I had allowed myself to become so enamored of the crowd that I completely lost sight of the individual. This constitutes a nearly unpardonable sin for anyone who claims the title of "pastor." Jesus said, "I am the good shepherd; and I know My own" (John 10:14). I had failed to fulfill the most basic characteristic of a good shepherd.

Julie referred to me as "our wonderful 'youth pastor' [who] only cares about his own little cliques." She hit the bull's-eye with that statement. I had become so wrapped up in running my program that I no longer had time to get bogged down in the individual needs of some hurting teenagers. I had indeed become "a hypocrite who preaches brotherly love and yet does not live it."

Julie perceived me as one who stands "above the world looking down." Somehow I had communicated to her a judgmental attitude.

What if I didn't agree? What if my friends assured me that she was out of line? It didn't matter. The fact that I created in her the perception that I am judgmental demanded that I respond to her by making it right. "If therefore you are presenting your offering at the altar, and there remember that your brother has something against you, leave your offering there before the altar, and go your way; first be reconciled to your brother, and then come and present your offering" (Matthew 5:23-24).

What's the next step in making it right?

3. Determine the areas of offense and, without projecting any blame, ask for forgiveness.
Three days after receiving the letter I spoke at the baccalaureate service for the graduates of Julie's high school. I took my seat on the platform and waited for my spot on the program. The school's "Campus Singers" came on stage and took their places on risers immediately to my right. I happened to glance over my shoulder to sneak a peek at the choir when my eyes focused on the face of . . . guess who? Julie had no idea that I was the speaker, and I had no idea that she sang in the choir. During my entire message, she sat directly behind me with her arms folded and a scowl on her face, communicating obvious displeasure. I have never felt such agonizing pressure in my life. Drops of perspiration beaded up on my forehead even before I began.

Naturally, at the conclusion of the service, every grandmother in the house wanted to grab me and snap a picture with me and her grandson or granddaughter. But throughout all the fanfare, I had one thing on my mind. When I finally got free, I made a beeline over to Julie and asked, "Would it be all right if I met with you tomorrow after school in the lunch area?"

I kept the appointment with Julie the next day, and she looked terrified. I sat down across the table from her, looked her in the eyes, and sorrowfully said, "I have come here today to thank you for the letter you sent me. I must admit that it was one of the most painful ones that I have ever received. It hurt so bad because I know that what you said is true. I have communicated to you an attitude of indifference and a lack of love. I have been insensitive to you over these past six months, and I have come to ask you if you would please forgive me."

Notice that I did not project any blame. I could have easily said, "I was wrong, but so were you. What are you doing in bed with another girl?" Such wording would have been the epitome of insensitivity and a cheap method of justifying, or at least minimizing, my wrong. Jesus stated this principle in this way: "First take the log out of your own eye, and then you will see clearly to take the speck out of your brother's eye" (Matthew 7:5).

Julie immediately broke down and wept like a baby. She had come to our meeting literally scared to death. She couldn't sleep the night before, she had been so worried. She thought that I was going to

MUST WE ALWAYS ASK FOR FORGIVENESS?

No. There are two broad categories of criticism. We can be criticized concerning matters relating to our character and behavior. The opening letter contained several choice examples. These must be dealt with.

We can also be criticized concerning matters of someone's personal preference. Someone may not like the tie I wore last Sunday. Someone may rip into me concerning my teaching style. Someone may not like my personality. These fall into the category of personal preferences. I do not necessarily need to respond to these, unless I desire to use the criticism as an opportunity to reinforce two thoughts—that negative comments of this nature should only be made to me, and that unconditional love accepts someone just the way he is, whether he flows with our preferences or not.

scream at her for daring to send such a letter to someone in my position. When she admitted that to me, I felt even worse than she did. I had so communicated a lack of love that she had become terrified of me. Great credentials for a youth pastor, right?

I assured Julie again that I was not angry with her in the least. In fact, I felt genuinely grateful that someone finally had enough guts and concern for me to confront me honestly when I needed it. I let her know that I wanted to try my best to express more sensitivity to her and to others in the future. I asked her to periodically let me know if she could sense the change in my attitude and conduct.

Julie told me that she forgave me. She gave me a hug and we left that afternoon as friends. This meeting only began a process of rebuilding a friendship that I had allowed to fall into ruin.

4. Determine the needs of the critic.

This letter represented a desperate cry for help from one very needy young lady. Did you look for clues to Julie's needs? Let's see if your list looks like mine.

I'm sure this sentence stood out as you reread the letter: "If all my friends were like you, I'm sure I'd spend many crying, lonely nights with no one to talk to." I have no doubt that she did indeed "spend many crying, lonely nights with no one to talk to." Julie felt completely unloved.

"I don't ask love or appreciation from you, Dewey, but I will gladly accept it if it is truly meant and from the heart." Have you ever heard a more honest and desperate plea? Her heart ached for love and appreciation from someone, anyone. My impersonal flier, beginning with the words "Hey, my friend," triggered a deep-felt reaction. Rightly so.

How about this line? "You wouldn't lose so many Christians in need of love to Satan." With these words, she admitted to me that she had fallen to Satan's temptations and had gotten herself involved in some pretty heavy sin. What had she done? Keep reading.

"Not that I believe in Satan. I don't even believe in God anymore." Her faith had been shattered during the recent months. This girl, whom God committed to my spiritual oversight, teetered on the brink of total spiritual disaster.

"The world contains many horrible things (as I have found out lately)." Personal pain radiates through these words. I didn't know what her parenthetical statement, "as I have found out lately," meant, but I felt determined to find out.

How transparent can a person become? Check out this line: "Even if I wake up next Sunday morning in bed with another girl. . . ." So desperately in need of love, so disillusioned by the indifference of her Christian friends and leaders, she accepted the only form of love being offered at the time—the perverted love of an impassioned girl. After a six-month involvement, Julie felt all the more lonely, guilty, and desperate.

The capstone comes in the next line: "I care enough about the people I love not to let them sit waiting for six months without a word from me." The key word? *Waiting.* For six months she had waited for me to approach her just to ask her how she was doing. In her insecurity and loneliness she frantically needed to know that someone actually cared. Tragically, the expression of love she so desperately needed from me never came.

5. Determine to meet the needs of your critic to the best of your ability.

Our meeting in the lunch area did not end my responsibility to Julie.

I determined to communicate a personal message at least once a month. I renewed my commitment to maintaining the personal touch with every person in my ministry, and much of the content of chapter 7 resulted from that commitment.

As we met in the days following our initial discussion, I was shocked to discover just how deep and serious the problems had become. I knew she required a great deal of time and attention in walking through the complex web she had generated. Feeling uncomfortable in giving any girl that kind of personal time, I explained to her my dilemma and her need to meet with a staff woman who could more adequately meet her needs.

Julie began to turn around 180 degrees. I thanked God that I did not follow my immediate impulse and trash her letter when it first arrived on that bleak day so many months ago. In light of my experience with Julie, the words of Peter took on a whole new meaning: "For you have been called for this purpose, since Christ also suffered for you, leaving you an example for you to follow in His steps, who committed no sin, nor was any deceit found in His mouth; and while being reviled, He did not revile in return; while suffering, He uttered no threats, but kept entrusting Himself to Him who judges righteously" (1 Peter 2:21-23). Unfortunately, I was not in the category of one who "committed no sin." Yet His example prevailed and His blessing resulted.

A FEW ADDITIONAL THOUGHTS

What should we do if, as we follow these guidelines, the person will not forgive us? You will find the answer in Romans 12:18: "If possible, so far as it depends on you, be at peace with all men." If you have followed the steps outlined in this chapter, you will have fulfilled your responsibility, having done everything that "depends on you" toward the one whom you offended. God requires nothing else of you.

Keep the door open, however, because you'll never know at what point God will succeed in softening the person's heart. He will often use pain, personal loss, or other kinds of pressure to get someone's attention. When He does, don't be surprised if your most outspoken critic comes seeking your counsel or support. Resist the natural temptation of closing yourself off to him while secretly rejoicing at his suffering. The Scripture clearly states, "Weep with those who weep. . . . Never pay back evil for evil to anyone. . . . If your enemy is hungry, feed him" (Romans 12:15, 17, and 20).

Are our critics always right? No! In fact, they may often be completely wrong. However, as I mentioned, the fact that I have created such a perception requires me to take the proper steps in clearing my conscience. It matters not that the something my critic has against me may not be true. He thinks it is. I must therefore properly respond.

What if the criticism comes to us second- or third-hand? Most of the time, unfortunately, it will. Very few people have enough guts to tell us what they think face to face. In these instances, we have two options: ignore the criticism, or approach the critic as a questioner rather than as an accuser. In other words, we should give the critic the benefit of the doubt, because the one who told us about him may have misunderstood or exaggerated what was really said.

We approach someone as a questioner when we say, "It has come to my attention that you have said this about me. I have come to find out if indeed you did say it." If the person denies it, drop the matter. If he acknowledges that he did say it, ask him, "Why didn't you come to me about this?" Then proceed to follow the steps outlined in this chapter.

Life is never easy, is it? Ministry is hard enough without people taking their shots. As a friend of mine once so eloquently stated, "They may be sheep, but they have teeth!" Perhaps we can now face criticism with a positive attitude rather than a negative one, understanding that while our critics may have meant it for evil, "God meant it for good" (Genesis 50:20).

CHECKING YOUR HEART:
A Personal EKG

1. When was the last time you were criticized? How did you respond? Did you view it as a positive opportunity or a negative situation? Did it result in the strengthening of a relationship or the disintegration of one? To quote a cliché, did you become "bitter or better"? Which, if any, steps did you omit in dealing with the criticism? Which steps can now be implemented as you seek to rectify the situation?

2. Can you think of any other relationships that have been destroyed because of criticism? Can you think of someone who has something against you? If so, rethink the accusations of your critic. Can you pinpoint any blind spots or attitudes of offense that you need to make right? Carefully think through the wording of your apology. Use the words I gave to Julie in the lunch area as an example if you need to. Because of the delicacy of these situations, memorize your words. And please, in asking for forgiveness, do not project any blame.

3. Are you ready to eat some humble pie? What blind spots need correcting? Have your critics succeeded in pointing out something about your character that you never saw before? You will need to place yourself under someone's accountability concerning the changes you desire to make. Who should this person be? Look for someone who will be honest, supportive, and willing to confront. Ask him or her to check up on you at least once a week.

Define your goals specifically. "I will become more sensitive to the needs of people" is too general. "Whenever I say to someone, 'How are you doing?' I will wait for an honest response." That goal is specific. "I will ask three people each day what I can pray for and then write their responses in a little notebook." That goal is terrific.

4. As you again evaluate the words of your critic, can you list the needs revealed in the criticism? Plan a strategy to help meet them. Certainly, not every need will be met easily. You will have to determine how much time you can commit to each individual. When the criticism comes from a member of the opposite sex, extra precautions will be needed. Pray for God's leading as you set your agenda in meeting your critic's needs.

5. What kinds of words do you say to others? Do you use words that edify, that they "may give grace to those who hear"? (Ephesians 4:29) Or have you become just as guilty as those who criticize you? If you're not sure, take some time tomorrow to listen to your words through the ears of the ones to whom you are speaking.

Would you feel built up if someone spoke similar words to you?

6. What kinds of words do the young people in your youth group speak to each other? Teenagers will reflect their leaders. Make an evaluation as a staff of each other's speech habits. Make this a topic of discussion at the next staff meeting. What changes, if any, will need to be made?

13

"I Press On"
Maintaining a Heart for Personal Priorities

"I press on toward the goal for the prize of the upward call of God in Christ Jesus" (Philippians 3:14).

"Therefore, my beloved brethren, be steadfast, immovable, always abounding in the work of the Lord, knowing that your toil is not in vain in the Lord" (1 Corinthians 15:58).

"I'd much rather burn out for God than rust out." So goes my friend's philosophy of life. Do you know what I told him? "Then I've got some news for you, Ted. At the rate you're going, you'll achieve your goal by the end of the year!"

When it comes down to a question of burning out or rusting out, I don't want to do either. How about you? Oh, I know—I've probably heard it a thousand times: "The devil doesn't take a day off." To which I routinely respond, "Oh really? I didn't know that he was your role model."

Let's face the facts: the relentless pressures of ministry can become a constant physical, mental, emotional, and spiritual drain on the system. Like long-distance runners, youth workers who finish strong have learned how to pace themselves along the way. Unfortunately, too many of our ranks run like sprinters while participating in a marathon. Tragically, their end can be predicted with alarming accuracy.

No one is immune from burnout. I should know. I've been there. Several years ago, during my tenth year of ministry, I experienced the sensation of wanting to walk away from every responsibility, never to return. I dreamed about a cabin in the mountains and sitting beside a slow-moving, rippling stream. I fantasized about spending the rest of my life isolated somewhere without any phone, car, people, problems, pressures, or demands. My heart became consumed with a desire to give up, quit, lie down, and die. I didn't want to see, speak to, counsel, or even think about another teenager again. A dark cloud of depression settled over me as I questioned my call to the ministry, goals, dreams, and life direction. The fear of failure gripped my innermost being as I considered the possibility that after giving my gut in ministry for ten years, I had accomplished absolutely nothing.

Overcoming burnout became, for me, a matter of survival. I had no choice; I had to conquer burnout before burnout conquered me. This chapter represents a section out of my own personal journal. The lessons I learned during those agonizing months have been recorded here for your benefit. May these words serve as preventative medicine for anyone who has yet to wallow in the quicksand of burnout. If you discover that you are already in the process of sinking further and further into its miry grasp, feel encouraged—there is a way out!

SYMPTOMS OF BURNOUT

What does burnout look like? We can identify several possible symptoms. Take a personal inventory as you move through the following list.

1. Ministry becomes a drudgery.

The passion that once burned in our hearts gradually diminishes into a barely flickering flame. Responsibilities for which we once felt a keen sense of enthusiasm now become a habit, fulfilled out of a sense of duty. Creative ministry degenerates into nothing more than a cold, mechanical performance.

2. We become unable to concentrate on the "big picture."

One of my students walked into my office the other day and asked, "What are you doing?" I could have answered his question with any of three responses. I could have said, "I'm grading papers," or, "I'm fulfilling part of my responsibilities as a professor at this college." But my answer surprised him. At the risk of sounding a bit maudlin, I replied, "I am helping to change the world."

Everything we do in ministry, no matter how mundane, has as its end goal the changing of this world. That is the big picture. When burnout hits, however, we will invariably find ourselves woefully blinded to the big picture. We will feel trapped waist deep in the muck and mire of meaningless minutiae, drowning in an endless sea of trivial pursuits, all the while hating every painful minute of it.

3. We experience "phonephobia."

A telephone consists of nothing more than a series of electronic connections encased in plastic. Yet I've met some people who have become deathly afraid of that little communication device. Every time it rings, they go through severe emotional trauma. Don't laugh. This happened to me. My home could no longer be viewed as my haven because anyone who had my number could shatter my tranquillity by intruding at will.

4. We become insensitive to the needs of others.

We get to the point where we simply do not care anymore. A young person might finally open up and share with us the most heart-wrenching story ever, only to generate from us a yawn while we secretly wonder how we can end this dialogue and get away.

This indifference actually results from a defense mechanism at work to keep us from going off the deep end emotionally. A human being can carry the aches and pains of others only so long. There comes a point when we reach a saturation level and we have no alternative but to put our hands to our ears and silently scream, "Stop! I don't want to hear any more. I cannot handle it!" When I hit burnout mode, I would do almost anything to avoid hearing about another broken home, abuse situation, abortion, runaway, or suicide attempt. I became a man at civil war within myself. I knew my calling was to be there when the young people needed me. But I didn't want to hear their stories. The resulting guilt and frustration became at times overwhelming.

5. We feel uptight.

We are ready to fly off the handle at the slightest provocation. The pressures build up while our energy levels diminish. Left unchecked, this situation may gradually transform us into seething volcanoes of hostile emotions.

6. We desire to walk away, never to return.

I know of one tragic instance in which a pastor did literally walk away—from his family, ministry, home, everything. He vanished, never to be heard from again. While this may represent an extreme reaction to a rather common problem, many of us have secretly harbored such desires in our own hearts, have we not? I will guarantee this: if we do not succeed in conquering burnout, given the right set of circumstances we will lose everything, one way or another.

CAUSES OF BURNOUT

Before embarking on a discussion of the solutions to burnout, we must first gain a firm understanding of its causes.

1. Overcommitment

Let's begin with the basics. Burnout most often results from an involvement in too many responsibilities. The inability to say no will destroy quickly and completely.

2. Lack of clearly defined goals

Have you ever taken a trip and found yourself lost without a map? Ministry will become equally futile when we lack an understanding of where we are going, how we are getting there, or the reasons behind what we are doing.

3. Failure to gain personal refreshment

Read Mark 6:31. Jesus admonished His disciples to "Come away by yourselves to a lonely place and rest a while." If Jesus' disciples needed rest, so do we.

4. Attempting to be something or someone we are not

Youth workers too often want to emulate another's gifts, talents, personality, style, or influence. Have you ever been compared to another youth worker? I have—often. Try this one on for size: After spending a week at a summer camp with my youth group, I was startled when one of my own young people came up to me and said, "Wouldn't it be great if the camp speaker could be our youth pastor?" Needless to say, his enthusiastic comment did wonders for my self-esteem!

A girl in my group came up to me and shared, "Last week was the worst week of my life. I was so depressed I considered taking my own life. Then I went to Bible study and it turned my whole life around." She made me feel like a million dollars. I tried to sound humble when I replied, "Hey, thanks. You just made my day." To which she responded, "Oh no, not your Bible study. I meant this other Bible study I go to."

Recently, I was with a friend in the lobby of a Sunday School convention when two girls saw me. One of them gasped and said to the other, "That's him. Seriously, that's him." Her friend encouraged her to come up and talk to me, but she was too timid. I've got to admit I was feeling a bit proud at this whole situation, and I kept glancing at my friend to catch his reaction. I whispered to him, "You just watch how I handle this. I'll instantly put them at ease." Finally the girls got up enough nerve and walked up. I smiled at them, and said, "Hi, girls." Immediately, one of them blurted out, "Aren't you Ron Walters?" My friend lost it on the spot while I died in humiliation. I'll tell you what—it doesn't take much to make us try to become someone we are not.

5. Poor advance planning

If you pounded on my front door and screamed at the top of your lungs, "Fire!" do you have any idea what I would grab first? My month-at-a-glance calendar! I paid $4.95 for mine; it has become a hundred times more valuable to me than that. I had to learn the hard way. By making commitments in isolation from everything else going on during the month, I placed myself in a position in which I felt like a drowning man gasping for breath, wondering if escape from my scheduling blunders was even possible.

6. Activity orientation vs. achievement orientation

When we live our lives on treadmills, burnout will always lurk in our busy but meaningless schedules. I have seen the pattern too many times: incredibly busy days, hectic evenings, feelings of exhaustion coupled with sleepless nights, waking up feeling even more tired in the mornings only to dash off to even busier days, etc., ad nauseum, (here's the killer) with nothing lasting to show for all of this effort. So goes the life of an activity-oriented individual.

7. Becoming a pressure person rather than a priority person

There will always be an overabundance of voices clamoring for our attention. Most will be asking for something from us. The majority will believe that their particular problems overshadow the importance of others and will therefore demand our immediate attention. Crises seem to abound. The "urgent" can crop up unannounced at any moment. How do we respond? If we live our lives moving from one crisis to another without any sense of a commitment to biblical priorities, we will burn out for sure.

SOLUTIONS TO BURNOUT

We've spent an ample amount of time discussing the bad news. How about some good news? Burnout can actually be avoided or overcome. It's all a matter of knowing exactly what to do.

1. Before taking on any new commitments, count the cost.

What will be required in terms of preparation time? How about time away from the family? Will this require an ongoing commitment or is this a one-time situation? Will your involvement contribute to the overall direction of your life, or is it extraneous to your life purpose? Make a commitment to your family that you will not accept any new responsibilities unless they are all unanimously in support.

2. Learn how to say no without feeling guilty.

We all know how to say no; we just say it to the wrong people. Can anyone please explain this? When someone asks for my time, I feel incredible pressure to say, "I'm there." Yet, when my own children want to play football in the backyard, I can say, "Sorry, I don't have time," so easily. How about you? It all comes down to this commitment: We need to do a few things with excellence rather than many things with mediocrity. Living by priorities demands that we say no far more often than we say yes.

3. Plan times of personal refreshment.

God established the pattern. The keeping of the Sabbath was not a bad idea. God put us together, and He stated that human beings need one day of personal refreshment for every six days of labor. Take one full day off per week and guard that day tenaciously.

Take a full vacation every year. Please don't make the same mistake I made. For the first ten years of my ministry, I took no time off. None. I allowed myself to become a workaholic and nearly killed myself and my family in the process. Not anymore.

Too many people take what they call working vacations. There is no such thing. The words *work* and *vacation* are diametrically opposed to each other. The disciples periodically needed to get away and rest awhile. We are just as much His disciples as they. Christ's command holds true for us as well.

4. Accept your gifts and your weaknesses.

"God does not need another Billy Graham. He needs a first Dewey Bertolini." My youth pastor's words have echoed in my mind since the day he uttered them. Why did I feel such pressure? I have no idea. But I had convinced myself that God could not possibly use me. I suffered from an acute case of spiritual inferiority. I honestly believed that I needed to say everything and do everything like Billy Graham. He became my focus. My desire to emulate him nearly became my demise.

We cannot possibly be anyone other than who we are. While we must certainly seek to correct our character deficiencies, we must learn to accept our unchangeable characteristics. We all differ in terms of our gifts, talents, backgrounds, burdens, personalities, etc. The wise and fulfilled servant of Christ understands these differences and learns to minister accordingly.

I was taught incorrectly in seminary. I was told to program around my weaknesses in order to learn how to develop them, ignoring my strengths since I already possess them. My professor called it "being stretched." During my first years of ministry, I nearly self-destructed because I fervently sought to obey that instruction. How foolish! I have now learned to program around my strengths and delegate according to my weaknesses.

Learn your areas of strength. Give yourself to those tasks in which you experience fulfillment and effectiveness. Honestly evaluate your weaknesses. Gather those around you who display strength in areas in which you are weak. This is nothing more—nor less—than the body of Christ in action.

5. Learn to think one month in advance.

When people ask for a commitment of our time, we need to consider not only the date in question, but also how that day relates to the other days of the month. Just last week I was asked by a good friend to speak at a weekend high school camp. The dates were open, but they fell in the middle of an extremely intense period of ministry. I am familiar enough with my system to know that I will need a break during that period. I had to turn him down.

6. Become achievement oriented rather than activity oriented.

We unfortunately live in an extremely fast-paced, pleasure-seeking environment. Fun, good times, thrills, and parties have become ends in themselves. Most people have learned to fill their lonely, empty hours with meaningless activities, getting together just to get together. Our young people get caught up in this lifestyle; so do we. Indeed, most churches have become activity oriented, their calendars filled with softball leagues and cookouts—just for the sake of having them. "Food, fun, and fellowship" has become the banner cry of today's typical church.

In the midst of all of this, God commands us to redeem, or buy up as a valuable commodity, our time (Ephesians 5:16). As you become achievement oriented, you will invest your time, giving yourself to those tasks which will produce eternal dividends. Before committing yourself to anything, you will ask the question, "If I get involved in this, so what? What of eternal value will result?"

Let me venture an illustration. For seven seasons, I devoted every Friday night from April through August to a church league softball team. I love the game and I love to play. And there is certainly nothing wrong with playing softball. But I must admit to you that after seven years of this, I asked myself, "What do I have to show for my countless hours of playing time?" I could only come up with a pretty pitiful answer: "A bunch of scars and three trophies. That's it."

For the next eight years I coached a high school girls' city league softball team. This involvement allowed me to meet 75 percent of the high school girls in my city because the overwhelming majority played in the league. (I also met 75 percent of the guys in the city since they came out to watch the girls play.) I fostered relationships with hundreds of unsaved teenagers, gained a total acceptance as a part of the youth sports scene in my city, reinforced my access to the school campuses, was able to lead several young people to Christ, and helped dozens of young people develop the character qualities of discipline and good sportsmanship. Question: Which involvement constituted an activity and which one constituted an achievement?

7. Become a priority person rather than a pressure person.

I have a little sign in my office that reads, "I will let no man control my day." We cannot allow ourselves to become slaves to the pressures people will attempt to place upon us. Priorities must dictate the order of the day.

Perhaps I can suggest a few guidelines. First, people must always take priority over projects. Ministry is first and foremost a people business.

Second, pray continuously for discernment. Some people have legitimate needs which must be dealt with immediately. This afternoon a youth pastor friend of mine called me for some counsel as to how to minister to a family whose nineteen-year-old son just committed suicide. If I had put that one off until tomorrow, my counsel would have come too late. Other times we will have a very difficult time in distinguishing the genuinely important from the frivolous. Yet I guarantee that everyone will say things like "urgent," "important," "ASAP," "Have him call me this afternoon," or "Tell him I'm standing here in the rain, waiting for his call at a pay phone." (No, I didn't make that one up.)

Third, don't feel guilty when you don't get everything done. The benefit of a priority orientation is in the fact that we are getting the most important things done first.

Finally, our families must always take priority over our ministries. Whenever we must choose between one or the other, our families must win one hundred times out of one hundred.

We have taken a detailed look at the subject of burnout. The questions before the house are these: "Now what? What if I am there already? What changes will I need to make in order to get out of it, or to guarantee I will never fall into it?" The effectiveness of our ministries hinges upon our responses to these questions.

Take your personal EKG and implement the steps and ideas outlined for you. Purpose in your heart to emulate the example of the Apostle Paul who said, "I press on toward the goal for the prize of the upward call of God in Christ Jesus" (Philippians 3:14).

CHECKING YOUR HEART:
A Personal EKG

1. Are you considering any new involvements? Do you currently have time to fulfill your present responsibilities with excellence? Does anyone in your family object to your increasing your involvements? Will this new opportunity flow with the aim of your life, or might it become a distraction? Learn to live by the principle "When in doubt, don't." Pledge to your family your commitment never to accept any new responsibility without their wholehearted approval. If you are single, find a godly person whom you respect and ask him or her to hold you accountable concerning your schedule. You will find much wisdom in the principle, "Where there is no guidance, the people fall, but in abundance of counselors there is victory" (Proverbs 11:14).

2. What are your goals? What are your priorities? Given the fact that you have a limited number of hours, to what do you want to give your time? I have chosen to give myself to my family first, the students at the college second, youth workers and parents third, unsaved young people fourth, and Christian young people fifth. I simply don't have time to speak at sweetheart banquets or koinonia Christmas parties. I don't do pulpit supply on Sunday mornings. I would not for a moment suggest that these activities have no importance; they simply don't flow with the priorities of my life.

Determine two or three dimensions of ministry and give yourself wholly to them to the exclusion of everything else. Commit yourself to doing a few things with excellence rather than many things with mediocrity.

3. Establish a day off each week and honor it no matter what! Which day will it be? Select one. Let people know that you will be unavailable on your day off. Unplug your phone and allow yourself to get away from it all for twenty-four hours.

Get out your calendar and plan a trip. Plan an extended vacation and plan two or three day-long or overnight excursions for the year. Grab a bike and go. Get in the car and take a drive through a forest. Throw twenty bucks in Amtrak's direction and check out another city for the day. Whatever you do, make certain that (1) no one knows what you are doing; (2) no one can possibly get hold of you; and (3) you are doing nothing that is even remotely work-related.

4. Have you evaluated your strengths and weaknesses? If you are relatively new in ministry, you probably have not. But don't despair! This becomes one of the most exciting aspects of ministry. Try your hand at a variety of ministries. Pursue whatever your heart desires. In some of your ventures, you will experience a great amount of fulfillment and the evidence of effectiveness will be overwhelming. Other attempts will end up in someone's book entitled "Don't Let This Happen to You." It's OK to try and fail. Much better to try and fail than not try at all. I recently saw a poster which summarized my thoughts perfectly: "Courage is not displayed in the winning; courage is displayed in entering the race."

Once your strengths and weaknesses have been determined, give yourself to those tasks which are centered on your strengths. Allow others to fulfill those areas of ministry in which you feel ineffective or for which you have no burden.

If yours is a classic case of spiritual inferiority, do a study of Hebrews 11. I've heard the chapter referred to time after countless times as "God's Hall of Faith." Not so! God has no such "hall." You will not find within the kingdom any hotshots or superstars—just common, average, ordinary people like you and me (1 Corinthians 1:26ff). Your study of Hebrews 11 will reveal some startling facts about some of God's choicest servants. Would you like a sneak preview? If I were giving an exam, this would appear under the heading *Matching:*

1. One of the greatest leaders the world has ever seen	a. Fell because of the lust he had for a woman
2. Enshrined forever in the genealogy	b. Adulterer, liar, murderer
3. Noted forever as a patriarch; a direct ancestor of Jesus Christ	c. Cold-blooded murderer
4. The father of faith	d. A prostitute
5. A man after God's own heart	e. An extortioner
6. Appointed by God as a judge in Israel	f. Lied about his wife, doubted God, committed adultery

If God can take such shattered, broken lives and use them to accomplish His purposes, you can be sure God can use you. Remember, He doesn't need another Billy Graham; He needs and desperately wants a first *you.*

5. Do you own a "month-at-a-glance" calendar? If not, drop everything and buy one. An investment of three dollars may save your family and your ministry.

How many nights a week should you spend at home? Which day in the week have you set aside as a day off? How many commitments outside of your normal routine can you accept in the course of a month? After answering these questions, place a check in the upper right corner of each date on which you would be available for "extracurricular" commitments. And please, stick to it.

Have you already overly committed yourself for any upcoming months? If so, list each commitment in the order of its priority and begin to cut from the bottom of the list. I hate to cancel things and so do you. But sometimes a cancellation becomes a matter of survival. If the person to whom you made the commitment has your best interests at heart, he will not only understand but will commend you for the steps you're taking. If he refuses to understand, he will be revealing an extremely selfish attitude. Sadly, some people are more concerned about the success of their events than they are about the well-being of God's servants.

Don't allow someone's selfishness to hold you hostage by preventing you from doing what you know you should. If you receive any criticism because of a cancellation, simply and humbly say to the individual, "I'm sure you are as concerned as I am about the number of youth workers who are losing their families or their ministries. God forbid that this should ever happen to me. This cancellation will help to insure that it never does. Thanks for understanding."

6. Are you an activity-oriented or an achievement-oriented person? It's easy enough to find out. Make two columns on a sheet of paper. On the left side, list everything you have done and everywhere you have gone for the past month as well as the approximate amount of time these required. On the right-hand side, opposite each item listed, write down anything that was accomplished as a result of your expenditure of time. Add up the total number of hours you spent in your various involvements, and determine if you got a fair return for your investment. Did you end up wasting more time than you invested? If so, you have oriented your life to activities rather than achievements. How will this change in the future?

7. Do you live your life according to your priorities or your pressures? If you find yourself struggling at this point (join the club!), why not begin using a "to do" sheet? Take a half-sheet of paper, number one to ten, and draw a line and two boxes after each number. Each evening, think through the next day and every task, responsibility, or appointment that must be accomplished. Write them down as you think of them. After you complete the list, determine which of the items is the most important. In the box immediately following it, place a #1. Do this for each task listed. You will now have every responsibility listed in order of priority.

In the morning, start with the most important task first. When you have accomplished it, check it off in the second box, move on to #2, and so forth. At the end of the day, make a new list for the next. The items which were not completed will go at the top of tomorrow's list. This simple method will ensure that the most important tasks are being accomplished in preference to the ones of lesser importance. This constitutes a priority orientation.

EPILOGUE
"We Do Not Lose Heart"

"Therefore, since we have this ministry, as we received mercy, we do not lose heart" (2 Corinthians 4:1).

The Revolutionary War began as a grass-roots movement among common laborers. Unrest pervaded a society in which the Redcoats ("lobster backs," some people called them) tightened their stranglehold on the throats of the townsfolk. Many small skirmishes erupted spontaneously. The folklore inspired by this generation of our forefathers has filled volumes.

Recently I heard yet another story. As a company of British soldiers marched through a field en route to the settlement at Concord, several men and their sons stood their ground. As the soldiers approached the human blockade, a shot rang out, men fired, horses ran, women screamed, boys fled, and blood flowed. The army marched through, the dust settled, and a fifteen-year-old boy came upon the body of his father—dead.

One of the men grabbed him. "We'll head them off at the bridge!" he screamed. The survivors of the battle took a shortcut and strategically placed themselves, poised for another fight.

Guns flared and more men died. For the first time in his young, fifteen-year-long life, a boy who had just lost his father shot and killed a man. Overcome with confusing and contradictory emotions, he collapsed to the ground and cried out, "I just want to go home; I just want to go home!"

Do you ever feel that way? Does your heart ever cry out, "I just want to go home?" Mine does. Sometimes I feel like a homesick soldier, wondering if the war will ever end. I felt this sensation again just the other night. A teenage boy . . . incest by his own father . . . a cry for help falling on deaf ears . . . a search for an escape with no way out . . . a gun to his head, a shot ringing out—a casket and some flowers. One of over 5,000 such stories this year alone. I just want to go home.

Youth ministry is far more than principles and programs. Youth ministry is a relentless warfare in which we battle day and night.

The future of our world and eternal destinies of countless young people hang in the balance. We have been called by God into the single most strategic frontline battle in the kingdom. We do not fight for some earthly king; we fight for the King of kings and Lord of lords. We fight for the One upon whom God has bestowed "the name which is above every name, that at the name of Jesus every knee should bow, of those who are in heaven [the angels, too numerous to count] and on earth [more than five billion of us now], and under the earth [Satan and his demons], and that every tongue should confess that Jesus Christ is Lord, to the glory of God the Father" (Philippians 2:9-11).

We fight for the One who promised, "Yes, I am coming quickly" (Revelation 22:20). We fight for the One who has already won the war! Therefore, "we do not lose heart" (2 Corinthians 4:1).

Jeremiah knew something of the agony of spiritual warfare. "I have become a laughingstock all day long; everyone mocks me. For each time I speak, I cry aloud; I proclaim violence and destruction, because for me the word of the Lord has resulted in reproach and derision all day long" (Jeremiah 20:7-8). Jeremiah "just wanted to go home." But he couldn't. "But if I say, 'I will not remember Him or speak anymore in His name,' then in my heart it [the Word of God] becomes like a burning fire shut up in my bones; and I am weary of holding it in, and I cannot endure it" (Jeremiah 20:9). Jeremiah knew something of a passionate heart for proclaiming truth to a generation in desperate need of a word from God. He did not lose heart.

But what if the flame is flickering? How can passion be rekindled once again? Consider this four-point agenda.

First, surround yourself with some unsaved young people. Go to a high school football game, volunteer to chaperone at a junior high school dance, sit in McDonald's some Friday night, and just watch and listen. Why? Because if you spend time only with your youth group kids, your vision can very quickly become myopic.

You don't need to feel conspicuous. Blend in with the scenery and listen to the kids talk. Ask God to allow you to feel what He feels, see what He sees, and hear what He hears. You will begin to develop a whole new appreciation for what Jesus must have felt when "He saw a great multitude, and He felt compassion for them because they were like sheep without a shepherd; and He began to teach them many things" (Mark 6:34). You will begin to understand why Jesus "saw the city and wept over it" (Luke 19:41). You'll sense something of the emotions my friend must have felt when he took me one night to a hill overlooking the San Fernando Valley. As we beheld the breathtaking view of what must have been millions of lights, he said to me, "Dewey, don't ever forget that for every light you see down there, someone has a broken heart."

Second, select two or three principles from this book and begin to implement them. No one can possibly do everything all at once. Don't even try. Just select the two or three most important based on an evaluation of your ministry. As these fall into place, you will be able to implement more ideas in the future.

Third, become daring enough to take some risks without fearing the possibility of failure. Every situation is different. While I have tried to include only those youth ministry principles which are transferable, the specific implementation of each idea will differ from location to location. Some goals will remain unfulfilled and some of your efforts prove ineffective. If you try something unsuccessfully, simply figure out another way. We have never really failed until we give up completely.

Finally, stay where you are. Instability has become the order of the day for young people, largely because their leaders are themselves unstable. The average tenure of a youth pastor varies from nine to eighteen months. This reality can have a disastrous effect upon a young person who takes a risk and opens his life up to his youth pastor. Stability must return to the ranks of the youth worker.

If ever a guy had a good reason for leaving his church, young Timothy had one. False teachers had permeated his church, the men were not assuming their place of spiritual leadership, the women were dressing immodestly, the elders were unqualified, the widows were being neglected, his gift was falling into disuse, he was timid, he was not respected because of his youth, and for good measure he had frequent physical ailments. What kind of counsel would you give him?

What did his father in the faith tell him to do? "You're in over your head, Timothy. Enough is enough. The people don't appreciate you there. The handwriting is on the wall. The time has come to move on to a different ministry." You won't find counsel like that in 1 Timothy. Paul wrote Timothy, "Remain on at Ephesus" (1 Timothy 1:3).

I can't read the mind of God, but I would be very surprised if His plan for young people included moving their leaders around every nine to eighteen months! Paul's word to Timothy is indeed God's word to us. You may be going through an extremely difficult time. Discouragement may have become the order of the day. Obviously, if the church leadership is requiring you to violate a biblical conviction, you should move on. If not, I would encourage you to "remain on at Ephesus." Running from a problem to "greener grass" is only a short-term solution. Working through a problem may take longer, but the benefit both to your young people as well as to your own spiritual development far outweighs the negatives. Fruit that remains (John 15:16) will result only from long-term ministry.

We began this book with a very powerful and penetrating question: "Would you tell me, please, why I should get up in the morning?" In a day in which our nation's youth face a horrendously boring existence because they lack a cause, we have been called by God to penetrate their culture and call teenagers to a commitment to Jesus Christ. What a glorious task! What an unspeakable privilege! What an undeserved honor! May God richly bless you as you strive to glorify Him. And may the day come quickly when we stand before Jesus Christ and hear Him say to us, "Well done, good and faithful slave; you were faithful with a few things, I will put you in charge of many things, enter into the joy of your master" (Matthew 25:21).

APPENDIX A

SAMPLE OUTLINE: TOPICAL MESSAGE

TITLE: Satan: His Desire and His Destiny
TEXT: Matthew 25:41, 46
THEME: Satan is very real and desires to influence the lives of as many people, including believers, as he can.

INTRODUCTION

- Satan is not a fairy tale.
- Satan is not some grotesque Halloween story.
- Satan is not the figment of someone's deranged imagination.
- To deny the existence of Satan is to call Jesus Christ a liar.

I. WHO IS SATAN? (Ezekiel 28:12-17)

A. He was created perfect (12b).
B. He was indescribably beautiful (12b-13).
C. He was the anointed cherub—he's an angel (14).
D. At some point, he rebelled (15).
E. He tried to market his rebellion by selling it to others (the term "trade" in verse 16).

II. WHAT SIN DID HE COMMIT? (Isaiah 14:12-14) The five "I wills . . ."

A. "I will ascend [rise up and occupy] heaven" (13).
B. "I will raise my throne above the stars [angels] of God" (13).
C. "I will sit on the mount of the assembly [a reference to the place from which Messiah will rule the earth]" (13).
D. "I will ascend above the heights of the clouds [the majesty and glory of God]" (14).
E. "I will make myself like the Most High" (14).

III. WHAT IS HE LIKE NOW? Perhaps the best description is a consideration of his names. Consider this sampling:

A. Satan—God's declared enemy (Revelation 12:9)
B. Devil—one who slanders God (Matthew 25:41)

C. Liar (John 8:44)
D. Destroyer (Revelation 9:11)
E. Serpent—deceptive and crafty (Revelation 12:9)
F. Lion—ferocious and destructive (1 Peter 5:8)
G. The evil one (Matthew 6:13)

TRANSITIONAL THOUGHT: I am not afraid of Satan because greater is He that is in me than he that is in the world (1 John 4:4). However, I do respect the fact that he is evil, crafty, and bent on my destruction (1 Peter 5:8).

Satan cannot touch you and me without our permission (James 4:7). In what ways can we give Satan permission to invade our lives with his influence?

A. Rebellion (1 Samuel 15:23. To be involved in witchcraft or divination is to willingly expose myself to the realm or power of Satan.)
B. Satanic entertainment (1 Timothy 4:1. Any medium of communication which openly mocks God's name, God's standards, or openly praises Satan is satanic.)
C. Drugs (Revelation 9:21. The word *sorceries* comes from *pharmakia,* which means to become enchanted with or get high on an outside stimulus.)
D. Sexual involvement outside of marriage (Romans 1:25. The phrase "the lie" [definite article in the original] is the same phrase mentioned in John 8:44 and 2 Thessalonians 2:11, both in reference to Satan.)
E. Satanic activity (Deuteronomy 18:9-13)
F. The rejection of Jesus Christ (Luke 11:23)

CONCLUSION: If you have become involved in any of the above, slam the door shut. "Resist the devil and he will flee" (James 4:7).

APPENDIX B

SAMPLE TOPICAL TEACHING SCHEDULE

JUNE 22: Summer Kickoff

BACK TO THE BASICS SERIES (Poolside Bible studies)
JUNE 29: Making the Bible Come Alive (Part 1)
JULY 6: Making the Bible Come Alive (Part 2)
JULY 13: A Survey of the Old Testament—What's It All About?
JULY 20: A Survey of the New Testament—What's It All About?
JULY 27: Handling Temptation Triumphantly (Part 1)
AUGUST 3: Handling Temptation Triumphantly (Part 2)
AUGUST 10: Giving Away Your Faith (Part 1)
AUGUST 17: Giving Away Your Faith (Part 2)
AUGUST 24: Principles for Powerful Prayer (Part 1)
AUGUST 31: Principles for Powerful Prayer (Part 2)
SEPTEMBER 7: Prayer Meeting for the Upcoming School Year

SPIRITUAL WARFARE SERIES
SEPTEMBER 14: Satan: Who He Is and What He Wants
SEPTEMBER 21: Satan: His Plans and Purposes
SEPTEMBER 28: Satan: His Doom and Destiny
OCTOBER 5: Satan: Dealing with Diabolos

WHAT DOES THE BIBLE SAY ABOUT . . .
OCTOBER 12: The Lament of the Lonely
OCTOBER 19: Dreading Disappointment
OCTOBER 26: The Battle over Bitterness
NOVEMBER 2: Winning the War with Worry
NOVEMBER 9: Boredom: What to Do When the Party's Really Over
NOVEMBER 16: Giving in to Guilt
NOVEMBER 23: No Bible Study (Thanksgiving)
NOVEMBER 30: The Purpose of Pain
DECEMBER 7: The Wonders of Heaven
DECEMBER 14: The Horrors of Hell
DECEMBER 21: No Bible Study (Christmas)
DECEMBER 28: No Bible Study (New Year's)

FAMILY SERIES

JANUARY 4: Prayer Meeting for the Upcoming Semester
JANUARY 11: "But Why Did God Give Me a Family Like Mine?"
JANUARY 18: The Bliss and Blisters of Parental Authority
JANUARY 25: Picking Up the Pieces: What to Do When the Family Falls Apart
FEBRUARY 1: Setting the Standard: God's Design for the Family

DATING SERIES

FEBRUARY 8: Why Date and When
FEBRUARY 15: "This Is It"—Figuring Out When to Say "Yes!" (Whom to Date)
FEBRUARY 22: How to Date (Part 1)—From Manners to Money
MARCH 1: How to Date (Part 2)—The Physical Aspects of Dating
MARCH 8: What Is Genuine Love?—Crushes and Commitments
MARCH 15: God's Timing for Engagement

A SERIES ON SUICIDE

MARCH 22: Physical Suicide
MARCH 29: Mental Suicide
APRIL 5: Moral Suicide
APRIL 12: Spiritual Suicide
APRIL 19: Suicide: Answering the Anguish

JESUS CHRIST: YOU-CANNOT-IGNORE-HIM SERIES

APRIL 26: The Virgin Birth: Myth or Miracle?
MAY 3: Tested and Triumphant
MAY 10: As One Who Speaks with Authority
MAY 17: The Proof Is in the Pudding—A Myriad of Miracles
MAY 24: "It Is Finished"
MAY 31: "He Is Not Here—He Is Risen"
JUNE 7: "If Anyone Comes after Me"—His Call to Commitment
JUNE 14: School's Out Party

APPENDIX C

SAMPLE OUTLINE: EXPOSITORY MESSAGE

TITLE: "And Such Were Some of You"
TEXT: 1 Corinthians 6:9-11
THEME: When a person places his trust in Jesus Christ, his life will change.

INTRODUCTION
- Matthew 7:21-23, one of the most terrifying in the Bible
- Problem: didn't understand the principle of Matthew 7:15-20, "By their fruits"
- Same problem exists today: Jesus Christ = fire insurance, nothing more.
- 2 Corinthians 5:17; 1 Thessalonians 1:9; Titus 1:16; James 2:26

TRANSITIONAL STATEMENT: This is the very issue Paul confronts head-on here: What is the evidence of genuine faith in Christ? Writing to a carnal church in the midst of a pagan society, Paul is concerned with the absence of change in the lives of some of the so-called Corinthian believers. What about you? Does your life give evidence of a genuine faith in Jesus Christ? This passage is as relevant today as the day in which Paul penned it. We shall consider . . .

I. THE CONCERN (9a)
A. The declaration—"The unrighteous shall not inherit the kingdom of God."
B. The deception—"Do not be deceived." Have we been?

II. THE CATEGORIES (9b-10)
Note: Each category of sin does not represent a one-time failure but rather an ongoing lifestyle. While this list does not claim to be exhaustive, it does represent every major type of moral sin.
A. Fornication: general word for sexual immorality. Specifically, refers to sex between unmarried people.

B. Idolatry: any worship of a false god and/or involvement in a false religious system. A wholesale denial of Jesus Christ as the only way into a relationship with God (John 14:6; Acts 4:12).
C. Adultery: a married person engaging in sexual acts with someone who is not his or her spouse.
D. Effeminacy: corruption of the male/female distinction. Includes any gender perversion such as transvestism or sex changes (Deuteronomy 22:5).
E. Homosexuality: absolute perversion of God's created order. God pronounces a resulting judgment in Romans 1:26-27.
F. Thievery and Covetousness: the presence of and the living out of greed. Slavery to a materialistic life orientation. Thievery is the action; covetousness is the attitude.
G. Drunkenness: substance use and abuse. General word referring to any inward high resulting from an artificial stimulus.
H. Reviling: destroying others with words.
I. Swindling: business fraud. Taking advantage of another financially.

III. THE CONTRAST (11)

A. No sin is too great to be forgiven.
B. Salvation results in a changed life: "And such *were* some of you."
C. The changes take place in three arenas:
   1. Washed: a cleansed life (inward change)
   2. Sanctified: a changed behavior (outward change)
   3. Justified: a changed standing before God (upward change)

CONCLUSION:

- A new heart = a new lifestyle
- A transformed life = transformed living
- Examine yourselves: Do you give the evidence of genuine saving faith?

APPENDIX D

SAMPLE EXPOSITORY TEACHING SCHEDULE

Introductory Notes:

- Keep every lesson intensely relevant and practical. Throughout the preparation process, continually ask yourself, "So what? How will this message impact the lives of my students?"
- When teaching junior highers as opposed to senior highers, keep the lessons shorter and speak with greater animation.
- You do not need to cover every verse of every chapter of every book. Select those paragraphs which yield the most timely insights for the benefit of the young people in your group.

JUNE 19: Promotion Sunday—Welcome in all the new students!

THE STUDY OF JAMES

JUNE 26: James: Setting the Stage (a study in the background)
JULY 3: What to Do When the Heat Is On (James 1:1-8)
JULY 10: A Treatise Concerning Temptation (1:12-18)
JULY 17: The Wonder of the Word (1:19-27)
JULY 24: The Fickleness of Favoritism (2:1-13)
JULY 31: Wanted: Dead or Alive? (2:14-26)
AUGUST 7: The Taming of the Tongue (3:1-12)
AUGUST 14: A Pastor's Plea (4:1-10)
AUGUST 21: A Vanishing Vapor (4:13-17)
AUGUST 28: The Misuse of Money (5:1-6)
SEPTEMBER 4: Closing Considerations (5:7-20)

A STUDY OF 1 CORINTHIANS

SEPTEMBER 11: Setting the Stage
SEPTEMBER 18: Distress over Divisions (1:1-17)
SEPTEMBER 25: The Causes of Carnality (1:18–4:21)
OCTOBER 2: The Priority of Purity (5)
OCTOBER 9: Losing in Order to Win (6:1-11)
OCTOBER 16: A Sin Unlike Any Other (6:12-20)
OCTOBER 23: A Marriage Made in Heaven (7:1-40)
OCTOBER 30: Grappling with Gray Areas (8–10)
NOVEMBER 6: Try This One on for Size (11:1-16)

NOVEMBER 13: The Lord's Table—Its Use and Abuse (11:17-34)
NOVEMBER 20: "Now Concerning Spiritual Gifts," Part 1 (12)
NOVEMBER 27: "Now Concerning Spiritual Gifts," Part 2 (13)
DECEMBER 4: "Now Concerning Spiritual Gifts," Part 3 (14)
DECEMBER 11: "If Christ Has Not Been Raised" (15)
DECEMBER 18: Closing Considerations (16)
DECEMBER 25: Christmas

STUDIES IN PROVERBS (A study of selected themes)
JANUARY 1: Setting the Stage—A Time for Resolutions
JANUARY 8: The Greatness of a Good Name
JANUARY 15: The Duty of Discipline
JANUARY 22: The Sloth and the Sluggard
JANUARY 29: The Envy of the Evil
FEBRUARY 5: The Wealth of Wisdom
FEBRUARY 12: "This Bud's for You"—A Study of Strong Drink
FEBRUARY 19: The Friendship Factor
FEBRUARY 26: Grief over Gossip
MARCH 5: The Sensations of the Sensuous
MARCH 12: The Folly of the Foolish
MARCH 19: The Glory of the Godly

A STUDY OF PHILIPPIANS
MARCH 26: Setting the Stage
APRIL 2: A Bleak Backdrop (1)
APRIL 9: A Compelling Contrast (2)
APRIL 16: A Passionate Appeal (3)
APRIL 23: A Pattern for Peace (4)

APRIL 30: Open Forum—A Time for Questions and Answers

A STUDY OF JUDE
MAY 7: Setting the Stage
MAY 14: A Call to Contend (1-4)
MAY 21: The Discerning of a Deceiver (5-16)
MAY 28: A Study in Contrasts (17-23)
JUNE 4: A Grand Finale (24-25)

JUNE 11: The School Year in Review

APPENDIX E

INDIVIDUAL SURVEY

Note: This survey has proven invaluable as a tool in helping me to pinpoint the specific needs of my students. The questions, listed at random, focus on eight major areas of potential turmoil (family, dating, friendships, morality, life purpose, self-esteem, bitterness, and salvation).

Every young person involved in your group can be given this survey. Meet with one student at a time and ask the questions, writing down their answers as they respond. Explain that the answers will be kept in the strictest confidence.

As problems come to the surface, you do not need to deal with them during the survey. Make a note of them for future reference. You can design your teaching schedule so as to address the predominant issues raised in this survey while you deal with individual situations at a later date. You will find that your young people will tremendously enjoy spending one-on-one time with you and will greatly appreciate your interest and concern for their lives.

1. Who runs your home?
2. Has anyone ever deeply hurt you or in any way offended you?
3. What kind of person would you like to date?
4. Describe for me the events leading up to your salvation.
5. Have you ever had any doubts about your salvation?
6. Most people fight on as many as three battlefields: thoughts, actions, and habits. On how many battlefields are you currently fighting?
7. If someone was to write a book about your family life, what would the title be?
8. How far physically should a person go in dating?
9. Describe the happiest day of your life.
10. Describe the saddest day of your life.
11. How does a person become a Christian?
12. What is the one thing you would like to accomplish the most in your life?
13. Do you ever think about dying? If so, what kinds of thoughts?

14. If you could be doing anything ten years from now, what would it be?
15. If you were standing in front of a mirror and could change anything about yourself, what would you change?
16. If you could be anyone in the world, who would you be?
17. What is the purpose of a friend?
18. When is a person ready to date?
19. Describe the best friend you ever had.
20. If a magical genie could grant you three wishes, what would they be?
21. If you could set any goal for yourself and you were guaranteed that you would be successful in achieving it, what goal would you set?
22. What do you like best/least about yourself?
23. If you were standing in front of God and could ask Him anything, what would you ask?
24. What is your greatest fear in life?
25. What do you lie awake at night thinking about?
26. How did you start coming to this church?
27. What do you like best/least about your school?
28. What do you like best/least about our youth group?
29. What changes do you think I should make in order to make our youth group even better?
30. How can I, as your youth pastor, and especially as your friend, best serve you in the future?

APPENDIX F

VOLUNTEER STAFF APPLICATION

NAME ____

ADDRESS ______________ CITY __________ ZIP______

PHONE ____

OCCUPATION ___________________________________

MARITAL STATUS _______________________________

BIRTH DATE ___________________________________

HOW LONG HAVE YOU BEEN AT THIS CHURCH? _______

1. Give a brief account as to how you became a Christian:

2. Why do you feel led to work with young people?

3. If you could do anything in youth ministry, what would you like to do? Give me your top three desires:

a.

b.

c.

4. What kind of ministry experience do you have?

5. What is your educational background?

6. What are your three favorite hobbies/interests?

a.

b.

c.

7. What situations have you had to work through in your personal life that you can use in ministering to young people?

8. Describe your devotional life:

9. Describe your family life:

10. In what ways would you like me to minister to you during the time you serve on the youth staff?

APPENDIX G

SAMPLE VOLUNTEER STAFF CONTRACT

I, ________________, agree to serve on the junior high school staff for one year, beginning on ______________. In line with the goals of the youth ministry of this church and the desires of my own heart, my areas of responsibility will be as follows:

a. I agree to attend both the Sunday morning and evening services, 9:00–10:15 A.M.; 6:00–7:30 P.M.

b. I agree to attend the Sunday morning "Campus Connection," 10:30–12:00.

c. I agree to attend the Wednesday evening Bible study, 7:00–8:30.

d. I agree to attend the weekly staff training meeting, Wednesday evenings, 6:00–6:45.

e. I agree to attend the staff planning meeting, the first Sunday afternoon of each month, 1:00–3:30.

f. I agree to attend one social activity (of my choice) each month.

g. I agree to oversee an accountability group of ten sophomore guys, personally contacting each one at least once a week.

h. I agree to oversee the music ministry of the junior high group, including the selection of songs, playing guitar, leading the singing, and involving the students and other staff in the musical aspect of the group.

i. Because of my desire to see social activities carried out with good purposes and with a commitment to excellence, I also agree to serve on the social committee, helping to plan and execute six social activities during the next year.

j. Finally, I agree to personally notify Dewey at least two days in advance if I must miss an above mentioned commitment.

Signed:

______________________	______________________
Jack Henderson	Dewey Bertolini

APPENDIX H

ACTIVITY PLANNING CHECKLIST

EVENT: ______________________________
DATE: ______________________________
TIME: ______________________________
PLACED ON CHURCH CALENDAR: ______________

GOALS:

1. ______________________________
2. ______________________________
3. ______________________________
4. ______________________________
5. ______________________________

FACILITIES: checked out __________ reserved __________

1. ______________________________
2. ______________________________
3. ______________________________

EQUIPMENT NEEDED:

1. ______________________________
2. ______________________________
3. ______________________________
4. ______________________________
5. ______________________________

FOOD: overseen by ______________________

TRANSPORTATION:

vehicle ______________ driver ______________
______________ ______________
______________ ______________

PROMOTION: overseen by ______________
skits __________ fliers __________ mail __________
announcements ______________ banners ______________
phone calls ______________ other ______________

SIGN-UPS: overseen by ______________________________

PROGRAM: overseen by ______________________________

speaker ______________________________

contacted? ______________________________

music ______________ song sheets/overheads ______________

games: 1. ______________ 3. ______________

2. ______________ 4. ______________

event ______________ time ______________

______________ ______________

______________ ______________

______________ ______________

______________ ______________

CLEANUP CREW: 1. ______________ 3. ______________

2. ______________ 4. ______________

WAITING FOR YOUNG PEOPLE TO BE PICKED UP:

____

(Permission granted to photocopy.)

APPENDIX I

MEDICAL AND LIABILITY RELEASE FORM

(Should be printed on the church letterhead)

NAME ______________________________ AGE _________________
ADDRESS ____
CITY __________ ZIP __________ PHONE (___)_____________
IN EMERGENCY, NOTIFY ________________________________
PHONE (___)_____________
DOCTOR ____________________ CITY ______________________
PHONE (___)_____________

HEALTH HISTORY:

Allergies:	__ Insect stings	__ Drugs	__ Other allergies
Other Conditions:	__ Heart condition	__ Frequent colds	__ Chronic asthma
		__ Hay fever	
	__ Frequent stomach upsets	__ Diabetes	__ Epilepsy
		__ Physical handicap	

If you checked any of the above, please give details (i.e., include normal treatment of allergic reactions): ______________________
____
____

Date of last tetanus shot: ___________
Name and dosage of any medications that must be taken: _____
____

Any swimming restrictions: __Yes __No
Any activity restrictions: __Yes __No
What restrictions? ____

Our church's insurance is only secondary insurance. If you have medical insurance, your carrier will be billed for medical charges in the case of illness or injury while your son or daughter is on a church-related activity.

Do you have health insurance? __Yes __No
If "yes," Name: ____________________
Policy Number: ____________________
Address: ____________________

"In the event that I cannot be reached in an emergency during the dates specified on this form, I hereby give my permission to the physician or dentist selected by the church leadership to hospitalize, to secure proper treatment, and/or order an injection, anesthesia, or surgery for my son or daughter as deemed necessary."

LIABILITY RELEASE

Every activity sponsored by this church is carefully planned and adequately supervised by mature adults. However, even with the best of planning and precaution, unforeseen events can occur. By signing this form, the parent or guardian agrees to assume and accept all risks and hazards inherent in church-related social activities. They also agree not to hold this church or its employees or volunteer assistants liable for damages, losses, or injuries to the person or property undersigned. The parents or guardians understand that they are signing for the minor listed on this form and the signature is for both a medical and liability release.

Parent or guardian's signature ____________________
Valid from September 1, 1989–August 31, 1990

APPENDIX J

RECOMMENDED RESOURCES

In this list I have included books that have benefited my life or the lives of people I trust and respect. While I do not agree with every statement in every book (I don't even agree with everything I *have ever said!), these books are listed because each one does contain principles that will prove helpful to the reader. I hope they will enhance your ministry.*

PERSONAL GODLINESS AND SPIRITUAL GROWTH

Bounds, E.M. *Power Through Prayer.* Chicago: Moody Press, 1979.

Bridges, Jerry. *The Pursuit of Holiness.* Colorado Springs, Colo.: NavPress, 1978.

———. *The Practice of Godliness.* Colorado Springs, Colo.: NavPress, 1983.

———. *Trusting God.* Colorado Springs, Colo.: NavPress, 1988.

Colson, Charles. *Loving God.* Grand Rapids: Zondervan, 1983.

———. *Who Speaks for God?* Westchester, Ill.: Crossway, 1985.

———. *Kingdoms in Conflict.* Grand Rapids: Zondervan, 1988.

Edman, V. Raymond. *They Found the Secret.* Grand Rapids: Zondervan, 1960.

Getz, Gene. *The Measure of a Man.* Ventura, Calif.: Regal, 1974.

Needham, David. *Close to His Majesty.* Portland: Multnomah Press, 1987.

Packer, J.I. *Knowing God.* Downers Grove, Ill.: InterVarsity Press, 1973.

Taylor, Dr. and Mrs. Howard. *Hudson Taylor's Spiritual Secret.* Chicago: Moody, 1979.

Taylor, Richard. *The Disciplined Life-Style.* Minneapolis: Bethany House, 1962.

Tippet, Sammy. *Fire in Your Heart.* Chicago: Moody, 1987.

———. *The Prayer Factor.* Chicago: Moody, 1988.

Tozer, A.W. *The Knowledge of the Holy.* New York: Harper & Row, 1961.

———. *The Pursuit of God.* Camp Hill, Pa.: Christian Publishers, Inc., 1982.

PREACHING AND TEACHING

Drakeford, John. *Humor in Preaching.* Grand Rapids: Zondervan, 1986.
Hostetler, Michael. *Introducing the Sermon.* Grand Rapids: Zondervan, 1986.
Jackson, Forrest W. (ed.). *Bible Studies for Special Occasions in Youth Ministry.* Nashville: Broadman, 1982.
Liefeld, Walter. *New Testament Exposition.* Grand Rapids: Zondervan, 1984.
Lloyd-Jones, David Martyn. *Preaching and Preachers.* Grand Rapids: Zondervan, 1979.
Robinson, Haddon. *Biblical Preaching.* Grand Rapids: Baker, 1980.
Spurgeon, Charles Haddon. *Lectures to My Students.* Grand Rapids: Zondervan, 1954.
Vines, Jerry. *A Practical Guide to Sermon Preparation.* Chicago: Moody, 1985.
Worley, Mike. *Brand Name Christians.* Grand Rapids: Zondervan, 1988.

Note: if you are interested in pursuing a curriculum series, consider these four excellent sources:

David C. Cook Publishing—The Pacesetter Series.
Gospel Light—a variety of curriculum series and resource books.
Harvest House Publishers—The LifeSources for Youth.
Victor Books—SonPower Youth Sources.

YOUTH CULTURE AND ADOLESCENT DEVELOPMENT

Baucom, John Q. *Fatal Choice: The Teenage Suicide Crisis.* Chicago: Moody, 1986.
Becker, Verne; Stafford, Tim; and Yancey, Philip. *Questions? Answers!* Wheaton, Ill.: Tyndale, 1986.
Carter, Velma Thorne, and Leavenworth, J. Lynn. *Caught in the Middle: Children of Divorce.* Valley Forge, Pa.: Judson, 1985.
Dobson, James. *Preparing for Adolescence.* Waco, Texas: Word, 1980.
Farel, Anita M. *Early Adolescence: What Parents Need to Know.*

Carrboro, N.C.: Center for Early Adolescence, n.d.
Koteskey, Ronald L. *Understanding Adolescence.* Wheaton, Ill.: Victor, 1987.
McDowell, Josh, and Day, Dick. *Why Wait? What You Should Know About the Teen Sexuality Crisis.* San Bernardino, Calif.: Here's Life, 1987.
Norman, Jane, and Harris, Myron. *The Private Life of the American Teenager.* New York: Rawson Wade, 1981.
Sanders, Bill. *Tough Turf: A Teen Survival Manual.* Old Tappan, N.J.: Revell, 1986.
Short, Ray. *Sex, Dating, and Love: 77 Questions Most Often Asked.* Minneapolis: Augsburg, 1984.
Stacey, William A., and Shupe, Anson. *The Family Secret: Domestic Violence in America.* Boston: Beacon, 1983.
Strommen, Merton P. *Five Cries of Youth.* New York: Harper & Row, 1974.
Wood, Barry. *Questions Teenagers Ask About Dating and Sex.* Old Tappan, N.J.: Revell, 1981.

RELATIONAL MINISTRY/COUNSELING

Adams, Jay E. *Competent to Counsel.* Phillipsburg, N.J.: Presbyterian and Reformed Publishing Company, 1970.
______. *The Christian Counselor's Manual.* Phillipsburg, N.J.: Presbyterian and Reformed Publishing Company, 1973.
Burns, Jim. *The Youth Builder.* Eugene, Ore.: Harvest House, 1988.
Collins, Gary R. *Christian Counseling: A Comprehensive Guide.* Waco, Texas: Word, 1980.
Crabb, Lawrence J. *Understanding People.* Grand Rapids: Zondervan, 1987.
Olson, Arvis. *Sexuality: Guidelines for Teenagers.* Grand Rapids: Baker, 1981.
Olson, Keith. *Counseling Teenagers.* Loveland, Colo.: Group Books, 1984.
Rinehart, Stacy, and Rinehart, Paula. *Choices: Finding God's Way in Dating, Sex, Singleness, and Marriage.* Colorado Springs, Colo.: NavPress, 1984.
Spotts, Dwight, and Veerman, David. *Reaching Out to Troubled*

Youth. Wheaton, Ill.: Victor, 1987.
Veerman, David R. *Youth Evangelism.* Wheaton, Ill.: Victor, 1988.
World Wide Publications. *The Christian Worker's Handbook.* Minneapolis, 1981.
Yancey, Phillip. *Where Is God When It Hurts?* Wheaton, Ill.: Campus Life Books, 1984.
Youth for Christ/USA, Youth Guidance Division. *Child Abuse and Neglect Handbook.* Wheaton, Ill., 1983.

MINISTRY TO PARENTS

Borthwick, Paul. *But You Don't Understand.* Nashville: Nelson, 1986.
Campbell, Ross. *How to Really Love Your Teenager.* Wheaton, Ill.: Victor, 1981.
Dobson, James. *Dr. Dobson Answers Your Questions.* Wheaton, Ill.: Tyndale, 1982.
Dockrey, Karen. *Combined Efforts: A Youth Worker's Guide to Family Ministry.* Wheaton, Ill.: Victor, 1989.
Johnson, Rex. *Communication: Key to Your Parents.* Irvine, Calif.: Harvest House, 1978.
Kesler, Jay (ed.). *Parents and Teenagers.* Wheaton, Ill.: Victor, 1984.
______. *Ten Mistakes Parents Make with Teenagers.* Brentwood, Tenn.: Wolgemuth & Hyatt, 1988.
Lewis, Margie. *The Hurting Parent.* Grand Rapids: Zondervan, 1980.
Narramore, Bruce. *Help! I'm a Parent!* Grand Rapids: Zondervan, 1972.
Ridenour, Fritz. *What Teenagers Wish Their Parents Knew About Kids.* Waco, Texas: Word, 1983.
Strommen, Merton P. and Irene A. *Five Cries of Parents.* New York: Harper & Row, 1984.
White, John. *Parents in Pain.* Downers Grove, Ill.: InterVarsity Press, 1979.
Wilson, Earl D. *You Try Being a Teenager.* Portland, Ore.: Multnomah, 1982.
Wright, Norman, and Johnson, Rex. *Communication: Key to Your Teens.* Irvine, Calif.: Harvest House, 1978.

VOLUNTEER YOUTH STAFF

Christie, Les. *Unsung Heroes.* Grand Rapids: Zondervan, 1987.

Holderness, Ginny. *Youth Ministry: The New Team Approach.* Atlanta: John Knox, 1981.

McDounough, Reginald M. *Working With Volunteer Leaders in the Church.* Nashville: Broadman, 1976.

Senter, Mark. *The Art of Recruiting Volunteers.* Wheaton, Ill.: Victor, 1984.

Stone, J. David, and Miller, Rose Mary. *Volunteer Youth Workers.* Loveland, Colo.: Group Books, 1985.

ACTIVITY AND MEETING IDEAS

"The Any Old Time Series." Wheaton, Ill.: Victor.

Benson, Marilyn and Dennis. *Hard Times Catalog for Youth Ministry.* Loveland, Colo.: Group Books, 1982.

Bimler, Richard (ed.). *The Youth Group Meeting Guide.* Loveland, Colo.: Group Books, 1984.

Hansen, Cindy (ed.). *Group Magazine's Best Youth Group Programs.* Loveland, Colo.: Group Books, 1986.

"The Ideas Library." El Cajon, Calif.: Youth Specialties.

Lynn, David, and Yaconelli, Mike. *Tension Getters.* Grand Rapids: Zondervan, 1985.

______. *Tension Getters II.* Grand Rapids: Zondervan, 1986.

Rice, Wayne. *Great Ideas for Small Youth Groups.* Grand Rapids: Zondervan, 1986.

Rice, Wayne, and Yaconelli, Mike. *Incredible Ideas for Youth Groups.* Grand Rapids: Zondervan, 1982.

______. *Holiday Ideas for Youth Groups.* Grand Rapids: Zondervan, 1981.

______. *Creative Socials and Special Events.* Grand Rapids: Zondervan, 1986.

Schultz, Thom. *The Best of Try This One.* Loveland, Colo.: Group Books, 1981.

Sparks, Lee. *The Youth Group How-To Book.* Loveland, Colo.: Group Books, 1981.

BURNOUT AND TIME MANAGEMENT

Burns, Ridge, and Campbell, Pam. *Create in Me a Youth Ministry.* Wheaton, Ill.: Victor, 1986.

Christie, Les. *Getting a Grip on Time Management.* Wheaton, Ill.: Victor, 1984.

Hansel, Tim. *When I Relax I Feel Guilty.* Elgin, Ill.: David C. Cook, 1979.

Hummel, Charles. *Tyranny of the Urgent.* Downers Grove, Ill.: InterVarsity Press, 1967.

Moore, Raymond and Dorothy. *Homemade Health.* Waco, Texas: Word, 1986.

Sanders, J. Oswald. *Spiritual Leadership.* Chicago: Moody, 1980.

Sparks, Lee (ed.). *The Youth Worker's Personal Management Handbook.* Loveland, Colo.: Group Books, 1985.

ADDITIONAL RESOURCES

Beltz, Dr. Bob. *Daily Disciplines for a Christian Man.* Colorado Springs: NavPress, 1993.

Cloud, Dr. Henry. *Changes That Heal.* Grand Rapids: Zondervan, 1992.

Crabb, Dr. Larry. *Finding God.* Grand Rapids: Zondervan, 1993.

Ford, Leighton. *The Power of Story.* Colorado Springs: NavPress, 1993.

Hicks, Cynthia and Robert. *The Feminine Journey.* Colorado Springs: NavPress, 1994.

Hicks, Dr. Robert. *The Masculine Journey.* Colorado Springs: NavPress, 1993.

The Life Application Bible. Wheaton, IL: Tyndale House Publishers, 1988.